EMOTIONAL FIRST AID MANUAL

JOHN THOMAS STEWART

Graphics by Susan B. Hunt

FIRST CANADIAN EDITION

Published by

The Canadian Mental Health Association
British Columbia Division

and

Para-Professional Associates

1985

FIRST AMERICAN EDITION

Published by

Para-Professional Associates

1985

Library of Congress Cataloging in Publication Data

Stewart, John Thomas, 1922-
 Emotional first aid manual.

 1. Crisis intervention (Psychiatry)—Handbooks, manuals, etc.   2. Psychiatric emergencies—
Handbooks, manuals, etc.   I. Title [DNLM: 1. Crisis Intervention—Handbooks.   2. Emergency
Services, Psychiatric—Handbooks.   3. Mental Disorders—Handbooks.   WM 34 S849e]
RC480.6.S74   1985   616.89′025   85-3718

Canadian Cataloging in Publication Data

Stewart, John Thomas, 1922-
 Emotional first aid manual

 ISBN 0-919104-46-0

 1. Crisis intervention (Psychiatry)   2. Helping behavior.   3. Counseling.
4. Volunteer workers in mental health.   I. Canadian Mental Health Association.
British Columbia Division.   II. Title.
RA790.5.S84   1985   362.2′04256   C85-091154-0

FORWARD

Dr. John T. Stewart began training volunteers early in his career as a rural pastor. During the period 1948 - 1955 he utilized volunteers in helping with the pastoral care of people in nine different communities in rural and urban New Brunswick, Canada.

From 1955 - 65 he trained volunteers who came from Bermuda and the Atlantic provinces of Canada to the Atlantic Christian Training Centre, Tatamagouche, Nova Scotia.

While studying in a doctoral program at Boston University from 1965 - 71 he worked as an intern at the Danielsen Pastoral Counseling Centre. In this period he a) developed a program for training volunteers as para-professionals in mental health, and b) worked part time on the staff of the Cape Ann Children and Family Center, Gloucester, Massachusetts.

He subscribes to the belief that adequate support systems are the best prevention and cure for emotional illness. He has a high regard for professional competency. He is of the opinion that an important role of the mental health professional is to provide training, support and supervision for volunteers and para-professionals.

He keeps in touch with his roots in rural Nova Scotia where he began his career as a farmer. In 1979 while on a sabbatical he laboured there as a logger for two months.

Since 1971 he has been the Director of the North Shore Counselling Centre, a Pastoral Counselling program serving the North Shore area of Greater Vancouver, British Columbia. The Centre staff provide therapy for individuals, families and couples. In addition they have trained 375 volunteers as first line helpers over the thirteen-year period.

More recently Dr. Stewart has been training first aiders in various communities in British Columbia on behalf of the Canadian Mental Health Association.

CONTENTS

Introduction

The decision to create a manual in the form of a book emerged in response to requests from the Canadian Mental Health Association for handouts for volunteers. At the time, I was training volunteers for the Association in various small communities in the Province of British Columbia, Canada.

Two major revisions were made to the original draft. Each revision integrated feedback from potential consumers, professionals and para-professionals, living in Canadian cities, towns and rural communities.

I would specifically like to thank Ron Brown, Joyce Evans, John Gray, Bob Horsfall, Kirsty Maxwell, Peter Newbery and Barry Stein for sharing their wisdom and experience. My special thanks go to Sue Hunt for her illustrations, Dani Kasburg for doing the word processing, Lillian Stewart for proof reading and Michael Kluckner for consultation.

I am most grateful for the support of Ron Brown of the Canadian Mental Health Association, British Columbia Division; without his encouragement the manual would still be an idea waiting to be created in art form.

It is my hope that this book will serve as a useful part of your support system. It is designed to be a helpful "friend in time of need". Pass on the good news by giving one of the tear-out order forms inside the back cover to friends who are helping people to help themselves.

I dedicate this manual to all those wonderful volunteers, often busy people who have been in my training programs in communities like Nashwaahsis, New Brunswick; Tatamagouche, Nova Scotia; Annisquam, Massachusetts; Hazelton and Vancouver, British Columbia; only to name a few.

John Thomas Stewart

PREFACE

A Note To All Caring People

The quality of life in your community depends in a very real way on you as a volunteer, on your personal qualities and on your competence as a helper.

One way to improve the quality of your own life is by providing appropriate competent help to your "neighbour."

This manual is for you if you are curious about the helping skills and personal qualities which undergird the successful outcome of counselling and therapy as provided by mental health professionals such as psychiatrists or pastoral counsellors.

This manual is for you if your situation resembles any one of the following:

Alice had offered her services to the local mental health association and was assigned to meet with a person who is now back in the community after a year in a psychiatric hospital. Alice is afraid of getting in "beyond her depth."

Carey lives in a rural community where there are practically no mental health services. Her children are all in school now and she has some interest in helping people. Recently she talked about her interest with the local doctor, a couple of teachers and a social worker who comes to the school one day a week. Carey knows that there is a lot of support in the community for many of the more fortunate folk. She is concerned about the less fortunate who have few friends and more serious emotional problems. She wants to know what will be involved if she makes herself available on a limited basis to a few of these people. She has a strong desire to get training in simple, but basic helping skills.

The local parish priest, **Father Brown**, has gathered together a small group of caring people to assist with pastoral care and to provide a network of support for people in the parish. Olive and Tom are part of the group. Talking about the project at breakfast they became aware that an issue of confidentiality had become a problem for one person they had visited. The group had not prepared them for this important issue. Tom needed to talk to the priest or someone who could help him with the situation. However, he had been asked by the other person "not to tell" anyone else.

Bill, unemployed for six months, is one of five volunteers who helps one day a week in a family life centre in a small town. In the past year, he has been to three workshops to learn basic skills. However all the ideas he has picked up haven't come together in his approach to helping others. He tries one idea and it works. A week later he applies the same idea again and it backfires. He ends up feeling that he doesn't know what he's doing and feels that he should leave well enough alone.

Edith does volunteer work at the hospital one afternoon a week. She's had some training in bedside manners on the wards. She's often at a loss as to how to respond when a patient starts talking about how upset he has been lately, worrying about supporting his family.

Elsie has been a full time mother for 15 years and is considering a new career. She is thinking about the mental health field. She is aware that this would mean years of college and clinical training. She has decided to become a volunteer as a way of arriving at a decision about college. She has been told that any experience as a trained volunteer would be useful in getting into college.

There are many popular psychology books available today in paperback editions. Much of their content focuses on self-improvement. At the other extreme are text books on mental health, psychiatry and psychology available as training or continuing education texts. Much of this literature in either of these groups will be confusing for the emotional first aider.

This manual is for you if you want to keep the personal touch in human relationships while more and more of life is dominated by computers and other high tech developments. So why shouldn't you read a manual, with a simple and basic approach to emotional first aid. Digest its contents, practice its skills and then use it as a ready reference.

Know and respect your limitations

THE PURPOSE OF THE MANUAL

It is not enough to assume that in emotional first aid situations the required help will be forthcoming from social agencies or from mental health professionals. With government cutbacks volunteers in the community are faced with doing the work once done by social agencies and mental health professionals.

The intention of this manual is threefold:

- To provide the emotional first aider with a resource when faced with specific problem situations.
- To serve as a self-training manual where organized courses are not available.
- To serve as a reference book for a course on Emotional First Aid.

The text's entire orientation is that of "helping people to help themselves." This emphasis on self-help is always within the context of a workable, available and adequate support system.

Professionals in the field of mental health have long emphasized that early, competent and caring help greatly reduces personal tragedy, as well as the cost to the individual and the community. A total of twenty-nine research projects in the United States show (1) that even one hour spent in psycho-therapy reduces medical care utilization sixty per cent over the next five years; (2) and six therapy visits can reduce medical care utilization by seventy-five per cent over the same 5 year period.

While the manual is not a primer for professionals, the principles herein have evolved from the experiences of both volunteers and professionals.

HOW TO USE THIS MANUAL

The most important first step in using this manual is to read and reread pages 17-30 which set out:
Emotional First Aid. What Is It?
The principles upon which Emotional First Aid is based.
The experience (process) of Emotional First Aid.
The Do's and Don'ts of Emotional First Aid.

There are four ways the first aider can use this manual.

- As a Trouble Shooting Resource.
- As a Self-Improvement Resource.
- As a Peer Training Resource.
- As a Text Book in an Emotional First Aid Course.

As A Trouble Shooting Resource

Trouble shooting is an excellent tool for the first aider;
- When facing a client who needs emotional first aid and the first aider is not clear about what needs to be done.
- When things have bogged down, or some serious breakdown has happened to the helping process and/or relationship in which the first aider has been involved.

In either of the above situations you would turn to the appropriate trouble shooting checklist after you have made some guesses about the nature of the problem you are facing.

Try it now to see how it works!

Here's how the Trouble Shooting Checklist works when the first aider is bogged down in a helping situation, for example, a 30 year old man you have been helping keeps asking for your advice, yet never follows through. You have become discouraged because he just does not take any steps toward solving his problem.

In this situation you would turn to the Trouble Shooting Checklist on challenging people to cope pp. **38**. From the list you would select those problems most like this one. You then turn to the appropriate pages in the manual. In the next meeting with the client you will follow the step by step procedures set forth in your selected section of the manual.

Chapter II has more on Trouble Shooting which includes five sets of checklists. [See the table of contents]

As A Self-Improvement Resource

All of Chapter IV and parts of Chapter V will be useful for those first aiders, para-professionals and volunteers who want to improve their helping skills.

The best time to do this is when you are working with clients. It is most helpful when used in conjunction with a client whom you are seeing over a period of several weeks.

Step by step procedure for using the manual as a self-improvement resource.

Step 1. Begin with;
The principles of Emotional First Aid.
The process (experience) of Emotional First Aid.
The Do's and Don'ts.

Step 2. During the beginning stages of the helping relationship, work your way through Part One of Chapter IV on Achieving A Relationship.

Step 3. Once your client's emotional storm has subsided begin to work through Part Two of Chapter IV on Boiling The Problem Down.

Step 4. When the client has clarified the problem(s) you then work through Part Three of Chapter IV on Challenging The Client To Cope.

Step 5. As you are motivated spend time on Chapter V about Special Situations. There are ideas and skills outlined there which are relevant to many helping situations.

As A Peer Training Resource

The steps to be used in Peer Training are exactly the same as those listed above for self-improvement. The big difference is that instead of learning alone you learn with the help of two other first aiders, para-professionals and/or volunteers. e.g.

You want to improve your listening skills. Find two others who are interested in improving their listening skills or some other aspect of achieving a helping relationship. Invite them to join you in a self-help group using the manual. Arrange times to meet. You will need at least five sessions, each two hours in length. It's best to allow for 8-10 meetings since there will be other skills you will want to practice.

The three of you will learn together through practice, discussion and reflecting on your skills.

Here's how you do the practice session.

Step 1. Select a helping situation. It's best to start with one of the illustrations. If you are going to practice your listening skills you can use the situation outlined on pp. 85. Once all three of you have learned how to keep strict confidentiality you can use a real life situation for practice.

Step 2. In the practice, one of you will be the observer, another the helper, and the third the client. There will be three rounds with each of you taking your turn as observer, helper and client.

Step 3. Arrange your seating so that the helper and client face each other and are at a comfortable distance from each other. The observer stays at a distance, only close enough to observe and to hear the conversation.

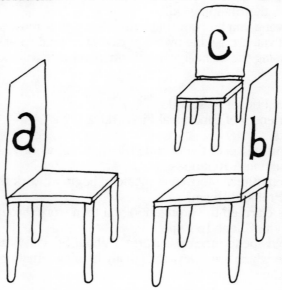

Step 4. Talk over each of the roles before you begin to practice.

The Helper (first aider)

This is the most important role. S/he is practicing listening skills. Don't get anxious about how well you do as the helper. You will learn most from your mistakes. Naturally you will feel good when the others affirm what you do well.

The Observer

The main task of the observer is to report back to the helper on his responses to the client. Be sure to include both the verbal (words spoken) responses and what you see; what the helper does, facial expressions and other movements.
The observer also acts as time-keeper. Stop the action after 5-8 minutes of practice.
The observer can be the discussion leader following the practice. Don't let the discussion stray. *Keep the focus on helping with skill improvement.* It's very easy to get sidetracked to discussing the client.

The Client

This is the *least* important of the three roles. The 'client' attempts to place him/herself in the shoes of the client. It's okay to be yourself so long as you a) stay with the client's situation, and b) try to express the feelings which you imagine the client would be having. Beware. *Do not* make things too difficult for the helper.
 Do not be too dramatic.

Step 5. Begin the role play (practice). If you are practicing listening skills, it would be best for the client to start.

Step 6. The observer stops the action after 5-8 minutes. Simply say "cut!". Then change seats so as to break from the roles.

Step 7. The observer reports on what s/he heard and observed about what the helper did by way of helping.

Step 8. The helper responds to the observer. It's a good idea to make mental notes about improvements you want to make.

Step 9. The client gives information about points in the practice when s/he felt a) helped (listened to in this case) or b) blocked, not helped (not listened to).

Step 10. If there is time discuss together what you learned.
Remember. When planning your time allow four minutes for reporting and discussion for every one minute of practice.

Step 11. Do it all over again (twice more) giving each first aider an opportunity to be the helper.

Warning

- Do not hurry this process. There is sufficient material in Chapter IV alone for twenty two-hour sessions spread over ten months.
- Remember that the focus is on helping the first aider, para-professional, and/or volunteer improve his/her skills. The focus is *not* on how well the client plays the role.

The Manual As A Text Book

The manual is designed for use as a text in conjunction with a first aid training package.
A guide for leaders to use with the text is available to workshop leaders by contacting the publisher.

Not all help is helpful

CHAPTER I

AN INTRODUCTION TO EMOTIONAL FIRST AID

INTRODUCTION

This manual is written from four basic perspectives:

a. The *best* emotional first aid helps clients to help themselves.

b. *First aid* in an emotional emergency situation is but a first step until professional help is acquired.

c. Increasing one's skills in emotional first aid is not a substitute for accelerated efforts toward improving social conditions and life styles.

d. Emotional first aid is a valuable service in situations where no emergency exists. It prevents emotional deterioration. As a non-emergency service it is valuable when the only qualified help available is through the first aider. In these situations the first aider acts in co-operation with or under the supervison of a mental health professional, who is not otherwise directly available to the client.

In the remainder of this introductory chapter we will look at:

Why you need this manual.
Emotional First Aid. What is it?
Why Emotional First Aid is important.
Who does it?
Emotional First Aid. It's language.
Emotional First Aid. Basic principles.
Emotional First Aid as an experience.
Do's and don'ts of Emotional First Aid.

EMOTIONAL FIRST AID - WHAT IS IT?

Emotional first aid is the assistance provided by helpers who are on the front line of where individuals, couples or families are suffering emotional pain, trauma or distress (usually in relation to some specific life situation). The concept of 'first aid' includes more than the idea of being first on the scene of the troubled situation.

The first aider may well be the first trained person on the scene, who is

- available in a private setting, office or home.
- answering a crisis call on the telephone.
- accidentally on the scene in a public setting.
- selected by a mental health professional for first line support.
- selected by an organization, such as a crisis centre or a church for first line support.

The first aider may be selected by the mental health professional to provide extra support in addition to therapy or counselling offered by the professional.

This concept of first aid includes para-professionals [other volunteers] who provide supportive counselling [on-going] to the emotionally handicapped.

In promoting the idea of emotional first aid we subscribe to the belief that much emotional pain and distress can be prevented by

- social action that help to change unhealthy community influences.
- encouraging people to adopt healthy life styles.
- practicing in our daily contact with peers, friends and family many of the principles set forth in this manual. e.g. *Helping people to help themselves.*

WHY DO YOU NEED THIS MANUAL

A revolution in mental health has been underway for a number of years now. In all likelihood you, the reader, are part of this dramatic change. The revolution I speak of is the extent in which volunteers and non-professionals are helping in the mental health field. While there are many text books available for the professional and plenty of pop-psychology books in the area of personal growth, there is no handbook which provides information and assistance for the volunteer or para-professional who is helping another person with an emotional problem.

If you are helping others with emotional problems you not only have a right to basic information about helping skills, but you have a moral obligation to know your limitations and to provide help which is helpful and is not harmful. There is no turning back the tide of the revolution by hiding one's head in the sand or by a general application of a half truth that "a little knowledge is a dangerous thing."

For those of you who are concerned about a lack of professional skills, there are two important principles which, if followed closely, will keep you from getting beyond your depth.

First there is the emphasis of helping the client to help him/herself.

Second there is a strong emphasis on knowing your limitations and referring to the appropriate professional, instead of trying to help beyond your competency.

There are a lot of mental health professionals who have worked as volunteers at one time, who now are trained and who are placing volunteers together with emotionally troubled people. These professionals also provide supervision for volunteers and para-professionals. They are aware of how necessary the information and help in this manual is. A few of these professionals will claim that "a little knowledge is a dangerous thing," however, a large majority of the mental health professionals *appreciate* you and your work so long as you do not try to help beyond your competency.

WHY EMOTIONAL FIRST AID IS IMPORTANT

Emotional First Aid is important because:
- of its availability when clients first need it.
- of its low cost compared with professional and/or institutional costs.
- people whose emotional trauma persists over a period of time are helped back to health through the resolution of their problem.
- the emotionally handicapped are helped by the first aider whose support is in addition to other support.

The first aider usually will be the first trained person on the scene when help is needed. It has been established with clarity through research that those clients who get help early in a crisis come through the crisis more able to cope with life than those people in crises who did not get help early.

The more persons available to people in crises is another very positive factor.

In certain small communities no trained help is available. The first aider will be the first person to get training for helping with emotional emergencies.

In many communities, large and small, clients often have to wait for weeks to get help. While the crisis may have passed, the unresolved emotions are repressed only to create problems later on for the client.

While the study of personal development and emotional growth is a new science, we know already certain important facts.

People under stress need competent others in sufficient numbers to 'help them help themselves' before emotional damage has taken place.

In 1970 the results of a study were published in a book "The Non-Professional Revolution in Mental Health." It is based on a study of over 10,000 non-professionals working in 185 mental health sponsored projects across the United States.

"The most frequently mentioned single reason for using non-professionals was the need to provide informal sustaining relationships to patients and clients."

"The next most frequently mentioned reason was the need to relieve the professional of tasks not requiring professional expertise."[1]

1 Sobey, Francine — *The Non-Professional Revolution in Mental Health*; published 1970, Columbia University Press, New York and London.

As we move forward into a more highly computerized and impersonal society, it is reasonable to conclude that your role as a first aider will become even more important than it is now.

The emotional well being, the mental health of individuals and families, the quality of life in your community all depend, in a very real way, on your competence, your personal qualities and your being appropriately available when people need help.

Helping people to help themselves

An Introduction to Emotional First Aid

EMOTIONAL FIRST AID - WHO DOES IT?

In order to be clear about the large group of people who do emotional first aid, let's divide them into four groups.

1) Volunteers who have had some basic training.
2) Para-professionals who are paid and who have responsibility for helping people who have emotional problems. e.g. A co-ordinator of volunteers.
3) Volunteers and/or neighbors without any training who find themselves in a situation where there is an emotional emergency and they have to do 'something' until someone with training is available.
4) Mental health professionals who find themselves dealing with clients who are in an emotional emergency.

Some first aiders in either category 1, 2 or 3 above may find that they have less than adequate training and are in situations [rural in particular] where no adequately trained professional is available to help when it is needed. These people are encouraged:

- to contact their local Mental Health Association or Centre for information about training opportunities.
- to use this manual as a self help tool until training can be acquired. See pp. 10 on How to Use this Manual.

First aiders will find work to do in one or more of the following situations. There may be other situations.

- As neighbors and friends.
- As volunteers whose authority, in part, is from a recognized community agency. e.g. Church, crisis line, Big Sisters, or one of the many helping organizations which emerged over the past few years.
- As paid professionals or para-professionals who find themselves facing a client in an emotional emergency.

There are not enough mental health professionals in our society to cover all emotional first aid requirements. Even if there were sufficient professionals, two obvious handicaps underlie the necessity for volunteer and non-professional help.

- The fact that first aid begins in the front line removed from the settings where most professionals work.
- The high cost of providing professional help *wherever* and *whenever* the need arises.

In summary, the manual is aimed at those first aiders who are in people's homes, at places of work or play, or who are helping clients in a more organized program within the community.

EMOTIONAL FIRST AID — ITS LANGUAGE

Some of the language of emotional first aid speaks for itself and needs no definition. There are about thirty words or terms used in this manual which will be either new to the first aider or will have their own specific meaning. These are defined below:

A.B.C.'s: A stands for "achieving the helping relationship"; B for "boiling the problem down" and C for "challenging the client to cope."

Acceptance: Is an aspect of the quality of the relationship wherein the client feels accepted by the helper.

Alcoholic: pp. 157 provides a careful and detailed definition.

Antisocial personality: This particular diagnostic term is included because of the serious difficulties in the way of helping such people with their emotions. Many of their emotional responses to life's situations are manipulative making it difficult to understand or to help them. The con artist is a prime example.

Attend: To give full attention to the person, to his/her feelings, words and expressions, hence the client feels the attention.

Client: A difficult helping word because of its association with customer. It is the common word used in the books in the helping field. 'Patient' is too medical, 'helpee' is too artificial.

Confidentiality: A quality of the helping relationship. The client has reason to trust *completely* that the first aider will not talk to others intentionally or unintentionally without clear permission.

Confront: Verbal questioning or encouraging the client to: a) look at things differently, to consider discrepancies in his/her story, feelings or behavior; b) change behavior.

Contract or covenant: The agreement made between the first aider and the client. It is assumed that there are always agreements, whether they are clear or acknowledged.

Crisis: An emotional emergency. The person in crisis is in danger of not being able to look after him/herself such as eating; or the person may be in danger of harming self or others, or in danger of an emotional collapse.

Defensive: The person who is emotionally defensive is attempting to solve his/her problem in ways which are usually unhelpful; some defenses are used against the help offered. Some defenses are helpful e.g. the defense of keeping a stiff upper lip when you are the only one around capable of taking charge.

Emotionally handicapped: See pp. 152 for details.

Emotional involvement: Refers to the first aider getting entangled in the client's emotions, usually out of his/her own unchecked or unconscious needs; e.g. feeling sorry for, or falling in love with the client, excessive worry about the client, getting angry with or at the client.

Empathy: See p. 90 for details.

Evaluation: A review of the helping relationship and process, and of the client's progress. Done at times during the process and usually at the end of a helping situation.

Helping alliance: The relationship that develops between the first aider and the helper. It describes a situation wherein the first aider helps the client to help him/herself.

Inter-dependent: Describes the quality of the relationship the client establishes with people who can help. It involves giving and receiving, appropriately being independent or dependent according to the circumstances.

Inner resources: Refers to the strengths for coping and managing life that the client has within, e.g. self-esteem, courage, humor, etc.

Judgmental: Viewing the client and his/her behavior with disapproval. This often involves disapproving not only the client's behavior but his self as well.

Network: Refers to the people in the client's and the first aider's support system. e.g. family, friends, peers at work and helping professionals such as doctors.

Para-professional: Refers to those people in the mental health field other than those professionals who are being paid for their work or services. The para-professional may be getting paid but is not in one of the mental health professions. e.g. a co-ordinator of volunteers. Usually the para-professional is a volunteer and may or may not be a mental health professional.

Process: The way the helping relationship happens. In particular it is what the first aider and the client see as the helping experience or journey together. An observer of the process may be more accurate in a description of what is seen.

Reality-testing: A check on how well the client is in touch with what is real around him/her. Is s/he aware of the time and day? Is his/her view of events greatly exaggerated or distorted?

Referral: Describes how the client gets to you or from you to another helper.

Repressed: Refers to emotions and memories of past traumatic experiences which have been put away, largely forgotten, but unresolved. These operate in one's unconscious often in ways which restrict one's ability to handle current and future crises.

Resistance: The client is dragging his/her feet in relationship to the help offered and available, often the resistance is not within the client's awareness.

Secondary gain: The benefits gained by the client through keeping his/her emotions or unhelpful behavior which appear to the client to be too valuable to give up, no matter how destructive. The client may not be aware that s/he is hanging on for reasons of "gain".

Supervision & Consultation: Both of these terms describe an aspect of the first aider's support system. In addition to support, these services are educational. In supervision your supervisor shares some of the responsibility with you and the contract is more ongoing and regular than in consultation.

Support-system: The same as "network" above.

Supportive counselling: Describes a helping relationship where the helper does not expect change or improvement by the client as a result of the relationship. The reality is that the client would likely deteriorate without the relationship. Any improvement would be incidental and a surprise.

Termination: The process of ending the helping relationship. One assumption of this manual is that it is unhelpful not to deal openly with the ending process.

Triangle: Refers to relationships where there are three's, usually three persons rather than three groupings of persons. e.g. The boss, the first aider and the client.

Unconscious: Refers to a large part of the individual's mental system, which is active whether or not one is awake. Often it is helpful for a client to develop awareness of some of the material and information in the unconscious. At other times a client needs help in repressing old fears or impulses which seem to have a way of breaking through into awareness and frightening the client.

EMOTIONAL FIRST AID — ITS BASIC PRINCIPLES

Emotional trauma, pain and turmoil are not always the result of accidents. This book acknowledges that some of the emotional trauma in our modern society is the result of unfortunate, unexpected crises, such as industrial or automobile accidents. Some of it is the result of the lack of nurture, love and support during the critical years of childhood and adolescence; some of it is simply the normal response of fairly healthy people to natural crises. *It is not the intent of the manual to focus on removing the causes*.

In the process of *'helping people to help themselves'*, there is a strong prevention aspect in that those people who have received help become better skilled and better equipped emotionally to handle their next crisis.

Getting emotional first aid as soon as possible in the crisis makes a big difference by way of lessening the severity of the crisis. The quality and type of the first aid further reduces the emotional severity and the length of the crisis.

This approach thus fosters good health and reduces loss of productivity, creativity and money by the individual, his employer and the community at large.

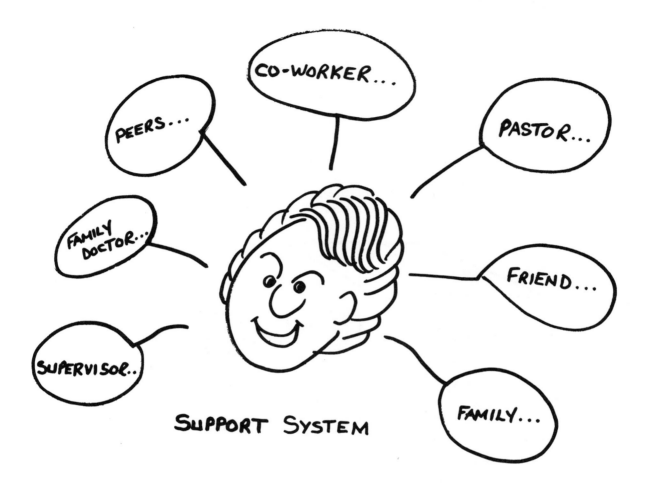

SUPPORT SYSTEM

The Principle of Having An Adequate Support System

With the mobility of people in the past fifty years, the networks of family and friends are so dispersed for a lot of people that they are of little help in time of need. In addition, more and more individuals have chosen to live by themselves. The result is that many people do not have the normal twenty-five other persons in their support system available when the crises come.

An important principle then is that the helper should do as much as possible to encourage and aid the client in building up an adequate and available support system.

EMOTIONAL FIRST AID AS AN EXPERIENCE

The process which the helper and client go through in the First Aid experience is one that moves from the initial introduction to the end, in progressive, clearly identifiable stages. This experience is sometimes referred to as the A B C's of helping.

The A B C Model was first developed as a technique for crisis counselling by a psychiatrist, Warren L. Jones.[1] The writer has adapted the model and has used it successfully for years after discovering it in a book *Pastoral Counseling*, by Howard J. Clinebell Jr.

'A' stands for the initial work and effort of Achieving a Relationship.

'B' Boiling the Problem Down symbolizes the next stage after the emotions have settled.

'C' stands for Challenging the Client to Cope; necessary in getting some resolution to the problem.

1   Jones, Warren L. — *The A-B-C Method of Crisis Management*; Mental Hygene (Jan. 1968), p. 87.

While there is some overlapping in the stages, you cannot do the work of B ahead of A, nor is the work of C effective unless B has been well done.

The final stage to the process is the ending of the helping relationship. We have included material on endings in Chapters IV and V.

A brief illustration outlining the process follows:

Jean is a trained emotional first aider. One Saturday she receives an anxious call from her old friend Elaine who asks Jean to come to see her neighbor Margaret whose husband has just walked out leaving Margaret with three small children. Elaine is afraid that Margaret will commit suicide.

Jean goes immediately; Elaine introduces her to Margaret (the client). Elaine leaves the scene for the time being.

During two hours Jean works on building a relationship with Margaret; the A part above. Trust develops and Margaret settles down emotionally. However, nothing much has been resolved.

Some work was done in relation to the B part above. Jean encouraged Margaret to take a look at the size and availability of her support system. During this process Margaret decided that she would call her sister who lived 40 kilometers away. She told her sister what had happened and the sister offered to come and stay for a day.

In this brief time together, Jean, the first aider and Margaret, the client, are already into the C part of helping, defined above.

Jean was able to help Margaret significantly over the next three weeks before dropping out of the picture. They did a lot of problem clarification together, B part above, as Margaret looked at her new situation. When Margaret felt overcome by her feelings they would move back into the A part for a brief time. At times, Jean had to confront Margaret in order to encourage her to follow up on some plan of action Margaret had thought of herself.

They ended the formal aspect of the first aid process when Margaret joined a self-help group for separating persons.

They accidentally see each other occasionally when shopping and stop to chat briefly. Usually Margaret reports something positive about her new life.

THE DO'S AND DONT'S

DO NOT

- Do not leak any confidential information to anyone!
- Do not make promises you cannot keep.
- Do not change appointments or be late.
- Do not argue with the client.
- Do not load the client with your own problems.
- Do not go along with deluded, unreal ideas or behavior.
- Do not encourage or suggest the use of medication other than what the doctor prescribes.
- Do not support clients when they disobey their doctor's orders and prescriptions.

DO

- Do take time to be courteous and friendly.
- Do be clear about any agreements you make with your client.
- Do try to understand what your client is experiencing.
- Do be completely honest.
- Do listen for feelings as well as for information.
- Do be supportive and encouraging.
- Do respect your client.
- Do encourage your client to take prescribed medication.
- Do keep your commitments of time.
- Do be trustworthy.
- Do remember that "laughter" can be good medicine.
- Do keep your own support system intact. Practice what you preach!

An Introduction to Emotional First Aid

CHAPTER II

TROUBLE SHOOTING AS AN EMOTIONAL FIRST AID

HOW TO USE THE CHECKLISTS

Trouble shooting can be a simple way of improving your skills as a helper as well as helping you turn a problem area into a creative experience in helping others. It is also a way of using this manual systematically and intentionally.

The trouble shooting procedures in this manual identify typical problems helpers experience in a variety of helping situations, and point to the specific page in the manual where there are ideas for help and learning. These are not the only approaches to your problem. There may be several approaches to a problem, but all methods offered in the manual have one common approach, 'helping people to help themselves'.

However, the trouble shooting checklist provides you with a systematic way of using the manual. You begin with your question or problem. The question may have to do with a specific problem you are experiencing in a helping relationship. Or you may have become aware that it is a recurring problem. If it's the latter, you need to focus on your role as the helper rather than on the client.

If the problem is an emergency, you would turn to the "Emergency" checklist, pp. 33.

If the problem is related to the helping relationship, you would go through that checklist.

If the client's problem is unclear, you turn to the checklist on Identification and Clarification, pp. 37.

When you are having difficulty in the area of challenging the client to 'get on with it' you go through the checklist on Challenging People to Cope.

A fifth checklist is provided to cover special situations.

Using the checklists for improving your skills

Those helpers who want to improve their helping skills may use the checklist in two steps:
1) As a means of identifying areas where you need to improve your skills.
2) As an index to discover where there is help for you in the manual.

Improving one's skills often results in increased satisfaction and enjoyment for the helper.

TROUBLE SHOOTING CHECKLIST

On Handling Emotional Emergency

TROUBLE SHOOTING CHECKLIST

On Achieving a Relationship

I'm worried about what to do when first meeting
the client. ....Check pg 87

The client sees me only as a volunteer and wants
someone with more status. ....Check pg 133
                                                                                                                    162

I seem to have to do all the talking. ....Check pg 87

I sense that the client doesn't trust me...................................Check pg 93

I ask the right questions but don't get any
information. ....Check pg 90

We got together once, but we don't connect and the
client appears to be avoiding any further
contacts...Check pg 92

We talked more about me than about the client and
I came away feeling that I was the one with the
problem...Chech pg 90

The client appeared to be experiencing something
which I could neither get in touch with nor
understand...Check pg 91

The feelings I pick up do not fit with the words
being spoken. ....Check pg 92

I doubt my authority as a helper. What right have
I to assume that I can help? ....Check pg 162

I'm uncomfortable because I'm aware that I'm
experiencing or have experienced problems similar
to the client's problems...Check pg 90

I don't like this client. ....Check pg 46

I feel that I'm getting caught in a triangle with
a family member of the client or with some other
person in the client's network. ....Check pg 95

TROUBLE SHOOTING CHECKLIST

On Boiling the Problem Down

"Problem Identification & Clarification"

TROUBLESHOOTING CHECKLIST

On Helping People to Help Themselves

Challenging People to Cope

I keep giving advice and the client doesn't follow
through. ....Check pg 85

I'm uncomfortable with the way and extent to which
the client is leaning on me. ....Check pg 102

The client doesn't seem to have other people to
relate to or to depend on for nurture. I feel
that I'm about the only one. ....Check pg 131

The client has little sense of self-worth and
confidence. ....Check pg 128

I'm having trouble understanding what support is,
if it's not giving advice or 'doing for' the
client. ....Check pg 26

I'm bogged down and need someone to talk to about
this helping situation (yet confidentiality is
important). ....Check pg 159

I'm burning out and find that I'm neglecting or
avoiding the client. ....Check pg 165

I feel depressed after a session. ....Check pg 166

We need to end the relationship, either because
the client doesn't need me any more, or I have
other priorities and I don't know how to go about
it. ....Check pg 141

We decided to end the relationship, but we are
having trouble letting go. ....Check pg 140

I need someone to help me improve my skills and
to check out how I'm doing, but I don't like the
idea of a supervisor or someone looking over my
shoulder. ....Check pg 166

I would like the client to use other resources
such as books, agencies, family, doctor, friends,
etc. but am not very good at this. ....Check pg 131

TROUBLE SHOOTING CHECKLIST

On Special Situations

It's difficult to do follow up with people I've
helped in an emergency...Check pg 147

Once the professional takes over, that seems to be
the end of both my responsibilities and
opportunity to help further..Check pg 147

When working with the emotionally handicapped, I
become impatient, take over and do their work for
them..Check pg 152

I find it hard to believe that teaching people how
to evaluate will improve their mental health...Check pg 136

I have difficulty in finding resources, telephone
numbers, and the right professional when my clients
need additional help..Check pg 145

CHAPTER III

HANDLING EMOTIONAL EMERGENCIES

INTRODUCTION

Emotional emergencies do happen. The growth in recent years of crisis telephone services is evidence of how common these emergencies are.

This chapter provides help for identifying emotional emergencies. It focuses on a variety of situations which are emergencies because there is danger to the client and/or to people around the client.

The following emergencies are covered with step by step procedures for handling them.

Acute grief   Acute anxiety
Extreme loneliness   Impending surgery
Danger of suicide   Violence
Child Abuse   Professional burnout

Getting professional help quickly in emergency situations is absolutely essential. We therefore provide a section on how to make referrals, pp. 46.

While the manual begins with emotional emergencies it does not stop there. Chapters IV and V are included to cover non-emergency situations because we subscribe to the belief that the first aider can provide an essential and valuable service where no emergency exists. Helping emotionally troubled people in non-emergency situations prevents further emotional deterioration. As with the Good Samaritan, it is not enough simply to bind up the wounds and then leave the injured.

An emotional emergency

WHEN IT'S AN EMERGENCY

Focus

Help in identifying emergency emotional situations.

Illustrations

A. A client calls in a crisis, her voice is tense and hard. She speaks rapidly saying that she is at the breaking point. She spills out at least three problems, one of them being anticipated surgery next week. It's two o'clock on Friday and many helping organizations will soon close for the weekend.

B. A widow and mother of a twenty-five year old daughter calls in a panic saying that her daughter's boyfriend of four years has ditched her and mother is afraid that her daughter is having a "nervous breakdown".

Comments

Emergencies are classified as situations where there is danger of further deterioration or of harm to the client or people around the client. Emergencies usually have the appearance of unfamiliarity at the onset of the emotional distress. Usually there is inability to cope with some aspect of life e.g. doing one's work, getting oneself dressed or looking after the children, etc. Often the client is afraid of cracking up, or afraid of harm from others or afraid of losing a relationship.

Because the client and maybe all those around are "cracking up" it is important that someone keeps cool. If the first aider becomes anxious and gets upset, the help offered may well not be helpful.

As a first aider, you may not have the luxury of sufficient time. In short, you will have to do your best in
- realistically and accurately sizing up the situation.
- getting the appropriate additional help needed for the emergency.
- finding out what you can expect the client to do for himself. By being calm yourself, this helps the client to cool down and more readily make use of his/her own strengths and skills.

It is difficult at times to determine whether the situation is an emergency or not.
- An emergency may be a situation where you are the only person at the time who senses that there is an emergency.
- The situation may be one where the client feels that there is an emergency and the client has initiated contact with you.
- A friend or neighbor of the client contacts you or brings the client to you, claiming that there is an emergency.

The emotional condition of the client provides you with information which helps in determining whether there is an emergency. Notable situations are as follows.
☆ The client is in a state of anxiety which leaves him/her unable to do basic simple tasks for himself or for those for whom he is responsible e.g. a mother in panic yet has the care of an infant. Anxiety attacks, sometimes sudden and severe are the most common emotional emergencies.
☆ Threat of suicide is clearly another emergency situation. Any threat should be taken seriously. Even those who don't really mean it, like wrist cutters and some people who overdose with pills, may have a suicide accident. This means that something goes wrong with their plan to seek attention or help only and they die as a result of the misfired plan.
☆ There are some depressed types who move back and forth between deep depression and extreme, even happy acting out. It is an emergency when this type withdraws his life's savings and goes off on a holiday to Hawaii.
☆ Lots of people for whom life is going along well and suddenly experience an unexpected loss, may react initially in a way which constitutes an emotional emergency. If a person is under severe stress and is responding in ways which are "out of the ordinary" for that person, it is likely to be an emergency.

Step by Step Procedure

1. Keep calm while assessing the nature of the situation.
2. Note who is saying that an emergency exists. Does your information come from your own observation and/or intuition?
3. Check the quality and availability of food and shelter.
4. Check for information which tells you whether the behavior is out of the ordinary for this client.
5. Ask yourself whether the client is faking an emergency. Is it a con job?
6. Is the client able to take care of ordinary responsibilities like getting dressed, etc?
7. Does the situation or atmosphere feel crazy to you?
8. Does the client know the time of day and day of the week?
9. Is there any threat of suicide?
10. Make an assessment of the client's immediate support system. Who are they? How available are they? How competent?
11. Take steps to involve others from that support system. Contacts should be made then and there if it's an emergency.
12. Get the client to a professional as soon as possible.
    Medical Doctor
    Psychiatrist
    The emergency section of a hospital
    A mental health centre
    A pastoral counselling centre.
13. If you have to leave, do *not* leave the client alone.
14. After the emergency is over, check back in order to do post emergency steps as required.

Bridging

These steps may also apply where there is physical injury and where the emotional aspect of the emergency is not very obvious.

Warning

- Keep calm. Remember your own resources.
- Do not leave the client unattended.
- Get professional help as soon as possible.

HOW TO MAKE A REFERRAL

Many helpers who work on the front line of everyday life, particularly the more competent ones, find that they regularly refer people to other helpers. I did a study some years ago which showed that the less competent and the poorly trained helpers tended not to refer. They also resisted turning to consultants for help in their work.

Focus

a. Improve your skills in making a referral.
b. Improve your skills in preparing your client so that there is limited opportunity for misunderstanding when the client and new helper meet.
c. Clarify what will be your most helpful role with the client during and after the referral has been completed.

Illustration

Elaine has been confused for a month now and you see no signs of improvement, in fact this morning she seems more confused and unable to make decisions. You feel certain that she should see her family doctor, perhaps even today. However, you sense that if you simply tell her what you think and then leave it to Elaine, she will do nothing. It is clear to you that Elaine needs help which is beyond your ability and training.

Comments

The majority of people who go to professional helpers are referred by someone else. Many of those with whom you work as a first aider will have been referred.

A common problem when the new helper and the client meet is that there has been some misunderstanding. Either the referring helper did not have the right information about the new helper, or failed to give enough information.

Another common problem is that the referring person conveys to the client all sorts of unnecessary anxiety about the seriousness of the client's condition. The client imagines that things are worse than they are.

A final problem is that the client often feels that the helper is simply getting rid of him and doesn't really care for him.

Biting off more than you can chew

Step by Step Procedure

1 Know your own limitations, your own feelings about 'possessing' your clients or about 'dumping' your clients.

2 Be able to make some assessment about the kind of help needed. Does this client need a psychiatrist or does he need a lawyer?

3 Find out whether the other helper can see your client. Get some idea about how soon.

4 Inform your client about details like fees, location, etc.

5 Always encourage clients who can cope to make their own telephone call to set up a time.

6 Check out the client's anxiety about taking this new step. Encourage the client to talk about the anxiety.

7 Go with your client for the first visit if this is appropriate.

8 If you are going to continue in a helping relationship with the client, it is an excellent idea for the three of you, the client, the new helper and you, to sit down together for a few minutes to clarify your helping roles.

9 Use the "ending" procedures outlined in pages 139 when terminating with your client.

10 Remember, if you take the trouble to follow the above steps, your client will not likely feel that you are dumping him. If he still feels that way, he can work on those feelings with the new helper. You have already demonstrated a lot of caring.

Bridging

The materials in this section are related to:
● the section on terminating pages 141-144.
● All situations where you refer clients to other helpers.

Warning

Be aware of any tendency on your part to *keep* clients, because:
● you are not familiar with referral procedures.
● you think that you are the only person who can *really* help.

There is no excuse for not knowing how to find other available resources in your community.

THE CLIENT WHO NEEDS PSYCHIATRIC OR SIMILAR MEDICAL ATTENTION

Focus

   a. Identify clients who need psychiatric or medical attention.

   b. Know what steps to take "until the doctor" comes.

Illustration

Arthur is a 40 year old man who has worked with the company as a bookkeeper three months. He seemed to fit in well at first. However, as the weeks went by, the other employees found him strange and overly suspicious. Two days ago, the division manager had a serious car accident and broke his leg. This is the second day that Arthur has been unable to focus on his work. He is convinced that the mafia was behind the accident and that they are after him as well.

Comments

Arthur's case is rather obvious, yet the 'suspicious' client can be quite convincing. Other kinds of severe disturbance are not so easy to identify. Every helper will face a severely disturbed person from time to time. You may even be facing a severely disturbed couple or family. When this happens, the helper needs some yardstick in order to know when s/he is in this situation, as well as some ideas as to what to do until adequate professional help is on the case.

Time to contact a professional

Some Clues for Identifying These Clients

- The helper has difficulty establishing any real contact with the person. The client does not come across as a "real" person. Emotional contact is very difficult. Often, but not always, the client presents a mixed-up picture of his/her world. Ideas will not be very connected. There is some 'craziness' in the room.
- The client has few on-going friends and a limited support system.
- The client presents imaginary ideas of either persecution or of grandeur; "being the world's greatest."
- The client has either hinted at or talked openly of suicide.
- The client is caught up in schemes and ventures in which s/he manipulates others, often in business transactions, does not pay bills, uses others and has no sense of guilt. (However, this client may fake guilt.)

What to Do When Found With This Type of Client

As a general rule, bring a second person into the meeting room in order to maintain reality and possibly as protection. Also, it is usually a good idea not to leave the client unattended or to send the client off to the next helper without someone going with the client. This suggestion does not apply to the manipulating client who has been operating this way for months or years.

Many of these severely emotionally disturbed clients do not need protection from themselves, however, I suggest that you do not take on the burden of deciding which of them do not need such care. *Leave that decision to the professionals*.

How to Help

The eager untrained first aider can easily get caught in futile attempts to help these individuals. Hence one can inadvertently contribute to the client's hurting himself and hurting (or killing) others.

1) The helper needs to develop skills in determining when a client is severely emotionally disturbed.
2) Once you are certain that there is severe disturbance or even if you tend to think and feel strongly that there may be, you need to take steps to call on the professionals.

3) You need to be firm with the client.
4) As a rule you should inform the client about your intentions (if there is danger of physical abuse, you may have to be devious in getting outside help).
5) At all times, let the client know that you care for him/her as a person. *Being firm, to the extent of going against the client's wishes or manipulations, can be caring.*

Step by Step Procedure

1. Once you pick up on the severity of the disturbance, inform the client of your need for external help and consultation. Be specific about whom you will contact.

2. Bring into the situation another person from your setting. Convey calmness and assurance that you know what you are doing. Communicate caring, gentleness and firmness.

3. As part of being ready for your task, you will have a list of available resources of professionals and their telephone numbers. A family doctor is a good first step. Make contact by phone with the most appropriate resource and tell him/her of your situation and what you want. Do not let the other person persuade you to take on more than you feel you can cope with.

4. Communicate to your client that you are ready to stand by to support until such time as the other support is in place.

5. Let your client know clearly what is going to happen next and that you believe that it is in the best interest of the client.

6. Turn to the chapter on referrals and endings, pp. 46. Beneath the client's unusual behaviour and thinking are fears and stress.

7. Be calm! Do not let the tense atmosphere interfere with your ability to help. Your client needs to feel your strength.

8. Quickly get professional help for your client.

Bridging

The principles, comments and procedures in this section apply also to situations where there is injury or sudden illness.

Warning

- Stay within your level of competency. Know your limits.
- Watch for your own burnout. See Chapter V, pp. 165 on The Helper Helps Himself.
- Do not be afraid to ask professionals for their help.

WHEN IT'S ACUTE GRIEF

Focus

a. Improve your ability to distinguish between emergency (acute) grief and normal grief.
b. Develop skills that will enable you to help the person who is in acute grief.

Illustration

Alice who is a devoted and very dependent wife and mother has just buried her husband. They have three young children. He died of an unexpected heart attack.

Three days after the funeral, Alice is:

☆ blaming the doctors for his death.
☆ talking seriously of leaving her children with her mother and going away to an expensive holiday resort for a month's vacation. Her mother is not well. It is not yet clear whether there are adequate finances for the future.
☆ complaining about heart pains and lies down frequently until the pain 'goes away.'

Alice has three symptoms of acute grief, the most obvious one that of developing the same symptoms from which her husband died. The other two, less obvious, indicate that an emergency exists.

An acute grief situation

Comments   Doctors, nurses, teachers, co-workers, ministers, priests or police are often the first people on the scene when an individual or a family has just learned of the death of a loved one.

A lot has been written about the grief process, yet little has been written about what to expect in a situation where there is acute grief and an emergency exists.

Let's look at the usual response to loss and death.

- There is some shock and disbelief.
- Sometimes there is a mixture of sadness and relief.
- A feeling of confusion is common.
- Worries about the future begin to emerge.
- Sometimes there is a temporary but mild inability to look after everyday matters, e.g. Filling the car with gas, etc.
- Some people experience some change in body functioning. e.g. Difficult breathing, loss of appetite or a heavy feeling.

All of the above reactions are quite normal. Abnormal grief looks somewhat different.

- Extreme and inappropriate guilt feelings.
- Ongoing inability to look after everyday responsibilities, e.g. Cook one's meals on a regular basis, dress small children, etc.
- Blaming doctors or nurses for the death.
- Denial that anything serious has happened and making inappropriate plans, like a vacation.
- Serious body dysfunctions which are new to the client, e.g. Loss of one's voice, paralysis of an arm. Sometimes these dysfunctions are the same as those experienced by the loved one during the illness.

All of these symptoms have a function, often misguided and destructive. They are uncontrolled attempts at avoiding facing

a) the loss.

b) the emotional pain which is a part of normal grief.

The first aider has a very important role to play in these situations because the *longer* the acute grief goes unresolved,

- the greater the damage.
- the more difficult it is for the bereaved to return to normal living.

All societies recognize the importance of "grief work" in that they provide community support and rituals to help the bereaved to work through their pain and loss.

The key role of the first aider is to get professional help for the acute grief victim.

The second role is to find whatever back-up is needed during the emergency part of the crisis.

Step by Step Procedure

1. Check for information both from the client and others to determine whether the death was unexpected.
2. Using the lists above, watch for clues to determine whether the client is experiencing normal or acute grief.
3. If it's normal grief, use your best listening skills (see pp. 85). Follow the steps for providing empathy, pp. 90.
4. If it's acute grief, follow step 3, but in addition work on developing trust, pp. 93, and persuade the client to see a professional. If there are body symptoms, the family doctor is the place to begin. If trust is low, begin with the priest or pastor who conducted the funeral.
5. You can offer your support by suggesting that you go with your client.
6. Often the family doctor, priest or pastor are not trained to help with acute grief. Do not hesitate in offering your observations to these professionals and suggest that additional professional help may be needed.
7. Reassure your clients all along. Tell them that sometimes these unusual symptoms go with grief, and that with help, they will soon be back to normal.
8. Make certain that the client has sufficient and caring other support people in his/her network. Sometimes there are too many people.
9. Encourage the client to carry on with the little, manageable everyday responsibilities.
10. Once the emotions have settled and the abnormal symptoms have stopped, encourage the client to slowly begin normal social activities.

Bridging

Symptoms of acute grief may develop where the traumatic loss is something other than death. e.g. Severe financial loss, separation, divorce, job loss, some form of physical disability.

Warning

- Do not take on responsibilities beyond your competency. It's a temptation when your client resists seeing a professional.
- Remember, delay in getting help is very serious.
- If behavior, however odd, is normal for your client, this is not likely an emergency.
- Mourning takes time.

WHEN THERE IS ACUTE ANXIETY

Focus

a. Improve your skills in distinguishing between normal anxiety, neurotic anxiety and acute anxiety.
b. Develop skills that will enable you to help the person who is experiencing acute anxiety.

Illustrations

A. Neurotic Anxiety

Elsie, at nineteen, has finished high school. She was planning to take a course in journalism several hundred miles from home. As graduation from high school drew near, she complained that something dreadful was going to happen. Through the summer she became worried that something might happen to her mother or younger sister after she left home. She was having difficulty getting to sleep and would waken at the slightest disturbance.

B. Acute Anxiety

Elsie is at college. It's the beginning of her second week of classes. She is having severe chest pains, trouble breathing, and has no appetite. Her roommate thinks that Elsie is having a "nervous breakdown." This morning Elsie is not able to leave her room either to go to breakfast or classes.

Comments

The most important first task of the first aider is to determine whether the anxiety is normal, neurotic or acute. While neurotic anxiety may develop into an acute emergency under extra stress, an emotional emergency does not exist.

Most of us experience feelings of stress and tension from time to time. Sometimes it is hard to know what it is about. Usually it goes away by itself or as a result of our having removed the cause. This is normal anxiety. e.g. Being worried about being late when the car does not start. We do not experience a storm of anxiety.

However, if the anxiety lasts too long and interferes with getting things done, then life becomes uncomfortable, we become irritable. We are not at our best either at work or at play. This condition describes neurotic anxiety.

Acute Anxiety is Noticeably Different

It is more severe.

There is usually a long build up, but the severity erupts unexpectedly. Some signs to watch for are:

Complaints of choking

Complaints of sweating easily

The mouth becomes dry

Breathing quickens and is shallow

Nausea or diarrhea may be present

Client may feel weak or dizzy

The client may have a lot of fear but does not know what s/he is afraid of

Most clients with acute anxiety only experience three or four of these symptoms at one time. If several of these persist after the obvious cause disappears or no reason is evident, then the client needs competent help to:

- relieve the anxiety
- protect the client
- possibly protect others
- prevent serious mental deterioration

The most obvious acute anxiety is when a person in the face of imminent danger freezes in his tracks. Such situations are not common. When one happens drastic and immediate intervention *may* be necessary in order to protect the client from physical danger.

Step by Step Procedure

1. Focus your attention on the client and try to get a feel for the client's ability for taking care of him/herself.
2. Check for signs of acute anxiety using the lists above.
3. Are the symptoms and behavior usual or unusual for your client.
4. Remain confident and hopeful. Offer realistic hope and assurance.
5. Take steps to involve others from the client's support system.
6. Do not attempt to help beyond your own level of competency. Arrange to get professional help for the client. e.g. The family doctor will be able to prescribe medication that will help reduce the anxiety.
7. When the emotional storm has abated you may want to involve the client in doing something about the cause of the anxiety.
8. If the cause is internal, this is best left to the professionals. It will take skill and time.
9. If the cause is essentially external, remember that the emotional crisis is internal. However, the approach in Part Two of Chapter IV will be useful as you apply first aid.
10. If the opportunity presents itself, involve the client in evaluating the experience of the attack. This will help to provide insurance against panic if another such situation occurs.

Bridging

Anxiety is a common emotional factor in every crisis. This section applies to the other emotional emergencies when anxiety becomes extreme and persists.

Warning

- When your client needs your full attention, do not spend time or energy trying to find the cause. A Dr. Menninger is reported to have said, "You don't need to know how a fire started to put it out."
- Do not apply the above steps and procedures to neurotic anxiety. This should be left to those professionals who are competent in helping with psychotherapy or stress reduction.

WHEN THERE IS EXTREME LONELINESS

Focus

a. Learn how to make contact with the extremely lonely people.
b. Identify real cases of extreme loneliness.
c. Discover how to motivate the client to build up his/her support system.
d. Avoid getting caught as the 'only one' in the client's support system.

Illustration

Leslie is a first aider in a small community. From time to time, he saw an older man walking down by the river. He had never talked to him but knew who he was. Out jogging one day in a light rain, Leslie found the man again and decided to stop and talk. To his surprise the man was in the same spot the next day. This time Leslie found it hard to get away. The old man just kept talking. He found that the man does not go anywhere socially and seldom talks to others except when he goes shopping.

Comments   The illustration above identifies several factors in helping the lonely.

- The emergency nature of the loneliness did not emerge at the first meeting.
- It is difficult for the extremely lonely to reach out to make contacts.
- Their support system is practically nonexistent. Family doctor and the clerk in the grocery store may be all there are.
- Having made contact, they may become clinging and possessive.
- The first aider may withdraw because of his/her own fears of getting caught.
- The first aider may not have skills in encouraging the extremely lonely person to build a support system.

The extremely lonely people have played some part (sometimes major) in creating their own loneliness. They may have a pattern of pushing people away or withdrawing while at the same time craving companionship.

They may have given up on asking and reaching out. TV may have become a substitute for real people.

Hanging on to "the good old days" often gets in the way of making new friends.

They may have difficulty trusting others, including the first aider.

Helping the extremely lonely person help himself requires skills in:

- Making the first contact with the client.
- Developing trust.
- Gently confronting the client to do something to change his/her life style.

Lonely people need encouragement to do an inventory of the size of their support network. How many family members are they in touch with? What friends do they have? How often are they in contact with family or friends? When the time is ripe, the lonely need to be confronted with the fact that the average person has 20-25 other persons in his/her support system.

We suggest that competent first aiders actively seek out the lonely because it is so difficult for the lonely to take the initiative and ask for help. The family doctor, the clerk in the grocery store or the apartment manager are often the only others they connect with in any meaningful way.

Every community needs appropriate groups and volunteers who have a concern for the extremely lonely people.

Step by Step
Procedure

1. Do not wait for the extremely lonely people to make the first move to ask for help.
2. Once you have made contact, take time to listen, pp. 85 and to establish trust, pp. 93.
3. Do some checking with the client to establish the degree of loneliness and the size of the support network.
4. Offer your services while being careful *not* to promise more than you can deliver.
5. Attach a condition to your offer which requires the client to work with you on building up his/her support network. See pp. 131 for suggestions.
6. If practical, add a further condition which requires the client to become part of some church or community group. Assist the client in doing some checking.
7. Ask around in the community for volunteers who want to help the lonely.
8. When you find a willing volunteer, introduce your client to the volunteer. Help them set up their contract. pp. 97.
9. End your relationship with the client when appropriate. pp. 139. There are others in the community who need your skills.

Bridging   The special skills required for helping the extremely lonely include many of the skills detailed in the A B C's of helping pp. 79-144.

Warning   The longer the period of time of withdrawal from others, the greater is the difficulty in helping the extremely lonely.

FACING SURGERY

Focus

This section can be used to develop skills that will enable the first aider to help the client who is having difficulties because of anxiety about upcoming surgery.

Illustration

Etta's family doctor had referred her to a specialist concerning a lump under her arm. The specialist tells her that she must undergo surgery. It will be 2-3 weeks before she gets into the hospital. She does not know whether it is malignant.

Etta belongs to a family that has a history of keeping such matters private and a secret. Her family doctor and her specialist have many demands on their time and cannot do much by way of listening to her unspoken concerns.

Comments

The anxiety that sometimes builds up prior to surgery can seriously affect the rate of recovery and the outcome of the surgery.

In the illustration, Etta is a prime candidate for an unnecessary prolonged recovery period. The build up of the anxiety will have a negative effect on the family's ability to function.

As a first aider, you may only get the opportunity to help when the situation has become acute. If it has become acute the section on Acute Anxiety pp. 55 will be of help.

Candidates for surgery may have concerns in one or more of the following areas:

- Fear of the unknown, especially if surgery is a new experience.
- Worries about practical everyday matters such as loss of income, care for the children, community responsibilities, work responsibilities.
- Fear of physical loss if the surgery has to do with body function or appearances.
- Fear of death.
- Fear of being unconscious.
- Fear of pain.

Where fear of death, pain or loss of some part of the body is involved, people tend to go through a lot of grief in advance of the event itself. The section on Acute Grief will help the first aider. See pp. 52.

Sometimes there is a lot of anger prior to the surgery. "Why is this happening to me?" "Why now?" If the anger is not expressed and 'let go of' the recovery and outcome will be difficult.

In the family itself there will be changes. An increase of conflict. An inability to carry out everyday responsibilities may develop. Some family member(s) may act out, e.g. drinking, stealing or skipping school. Let's see what the first aider can do.

Step by Step Procedure

1. Focus on building trust and guaranteeing confidentiality. See pp. 159.
2. Check and verify whether the signs and behavior are unusal for your client.
3. Remain confident and hopeful. Offer *realistic* hope and assurance.
4. Encourage your client to tell you about those concerns s/he has which can be relieved with more information. e.g. What to expect in the hospital after surgery.
5. Help your client to explore ways s/he can get this information. See pp. 126 on confronting a client.
6. Focus on helping the client to build up external resources. See pp. 131. Explore the availability of home makers, or other services. Encourage the client to make his/her own contacts if these services are needed.
7. Do not attempt to help beyond your own level of competency or the time you have available. Arrange to get professional help when needed.
8. If appropriate, accompany your client to the place where the needed information is available. e.g. family doctor, cancer clinic, social service department at the hospital.

Bridging

This material will be useful in situations where there are other forms of acute anxiety or grief before the event.

Warning

- Do not provide medical information in any attempts to reassure or inform the client.
- If the client is dwelling on a lot of old experiences of surgery, a professional can best help with the old unresolved emotional material.

THE TRAUMA OF ACCIDENTS

Focus

a. Identify when emotional first aid is appropriate when a client has been involved in a serious accident.

b. Identify which particular steps to take when applying emotional first aid to an accident victim.

Illustration

You are skiing and suddenly come upon two other skiers. One of them, Edna, is stretched out on the snow in great pain. The twisted leg looks like it might be broken. Her friend has released the binding but is in a panic and doesn't know what to do next and only sits there crying.

Edna looks very pale and has vomited. You see by her eyes that she is very frightened. She is suffering from:

● Physical injury and pain.

● A condition of shock.

What are your responsibilities as an emotional first aider?

Comments   Fear, anxiety and guilt are emotions which might quickly overwhelm an accident victim. The responsibilities of the first aider in the illustration are as follows:

☆ The first, is to sustain life. Do this in keeping with the best first aid skills taught in the St. John Ambulance course or in the Emergency First Aid Manual.

☆ The second responsibility is to prevent the physical condition from becoming worse. The St. John Ambulance manual is helpful.

☆ The third responsibility is to prevent the condition from becoming worse by attending to the client's fear and anxiety.

☆ The fourth is to provide post emergency follow up as a way of promoting recovery. The emotional issues at this stage include one or more of the following:

Anxiety   Loss of self-confidence

Loss or grief   Feelings of confusion

Fear of the future in the face of a different life situation. e.g. Loss of an arm.

It is important for the first aider to determine whether the client tended to be anxious prior to the accident. If so, it's best to leave the anxiety to a professional. However, if the anxiety is new and directly the result of the accident, the first aider can help through:

● Encouragement

● Reassurance

● Listening

● Helping the client to take action steps. See pp. 126.

The main points to remember regardless of which of the above responsibilities you are carrying out are:

Keep calm

Be supportive

Don't go beyond your competency.

**Step by Step
Procedure**

1. Keep calm.
2. Attend to those necessities for sustaining the victim's life. Send for medical help. Secure emergency first aid if you do not know what to do.
3. Do whatever is necessary to keep the victim's physical condition from becoming worse. e.g. Protect the victim from extreme cold.
4. Attend to the client's fear and anxiety while doing steps 2 and 3. Be reassuring. Tell your client what to expect next, and what you have done to secure additional help. See pp. 55 for steps in dealing with Acute Anxiety.
5. After the emergency has been taken care of through medical attention, contact the client and/or family to offer your help with post emergency service. Whatever effective help you can give in reducing their anxiety will go a long way toward promoting the victim's recovery.
6. During the post emergency period, whenever the need is beyond your level of competency, refer the client for professional help. See pp. 46.

Bridging

Parts One, Two and Three of Chapter IV will be useful when you become involved in post emergency follow up.

Warning

Remember that your own anxiety and fear may offset your best efforts to save the client's life. Keep calm and be sensitive to the client's emotional needs when you first enter the emergency situation.

WHEN THERE IS VIOLENCE

Focus

a. Develop skills in preventing further abuse when there is violence.
b. Develop skills in providing emotional first aid to:
   the victim
   the other family members
   the offender.
c. Become aware of legal responsibilities.

Illustration

Doris admitted herself to the outpatient department of the local hospital, fearing that she had broken ribs. Her spouse had beaten her. She does not want to involve the police. Someone told her about your first aid service and she asks the hospital attendant to call you.

You talk with Doris following her x-rays and find that,
- she can be released now.
- the offender is at home with the small children.
- that the offender had been drinking.

The nurse in charge tells you that there is a transition house for women and children in another town 35 miles away. How can you help?

Comments

Domestic violence is no respecter of social class or of professions. Domestic violence has more to do with:
   Family background and patterns
   Lack of ethics about physical abuse
   Frustration
   Drinking and drug abuse.
Because the patterns are well-established and long-standing they are difficult to change.

Violence usually involves a love-hate relationship in which the abused has a pattern of getting affection via the beating. Hence it is difficult for the spouse to lay a charge. Going to or calling the police is often part of the fighting. The spouse refuses to lay charges that might mean separation from the offender.

Women who are victims usually need a lot of rebuilding. Hence counselling by a first aider *is not* appropriate. The best rebuilding takes place in community, such as a transition house.

Women who have a grudge against men or men who have a grudge against women will *not* be helpful to either the victim or the offender. These highly motivated helpers will make things worse.

If the offender wants to talk, it is appropriate for the first aider to go to him and to talk with him about getting therapy.

The ideal setting for helping a family where violence is a pattern is in some sort of community or group where the following can be provided:

Lots of support

Supervision

Training in better ways to handle frustration

Training in better ways to give and get affection.

The usual domestic violent situation to expect includes:
- The call will come from the hospital, crisis line or from the victim. Sometimes it will come from a friend or neighbor of the victim.
- At the scene of the abuse the first aider will find that the woman has left the house.
- Alcohol will be involved and/or
- Drugs will be involved.
- The victim does not lay charges.
- There is severe psychological abuse, often on both sides.

Legal Aspects

In many provinces and states, charges are not laid unless the victim makes them.

When Trying to Help is Useless

☆ Trying to reason or argue with either the offender or the victim who is under the influence of alcohol or drugs.
☆ When the first aider is feeling a lot of anger about the situation.
☆ When the first aider takes sides.

When Trying to Help is Dangerous

It is *very dangerous* when the offender and the victim are actually fighting. It is common for one or both to turn on the helper.

Where Help is Available

Transition houses have become available in most larger centres. Telephone numbers are listed, but addresses are never publicized. Contact a crisis line, the police, hospital outpatient, human resources department of the government.

Handling Emotional Emergencies

Step by Step
Procedure

1. Keep calm and size up the situation.
2. Look for alcohol or drug involvement. Do not reason or argue with the client who is under the influence.
3. If the couple is fighting, stay away and get help. e.g. Call the police.
4. If the couple has stopped fighting, check to see if medical attention is needed and refer to a doctor or hospital outpatient.
5. If there is danger that the situation will deteriorate, take steps to remove the victim from the scene. Go to a transition house but do not give the address to the family. Inform the police if necessary.
6. Recommend on-going counselling to the client. If there is no transition house available, offer to assist the client in finding professional help.
7. Offer your help to the offender. Ask him if he wants to talk. The point of your help is to encourage him to get professional counselling.
8. Check with the clients in post-emergency follow up. See pp. 147. Most couples will be back in the family home once the emergency is over and without having improved.
9. During the post emergency support period, your goal is to encourage the family to get involved in a counselling program. See pp. 46 on making referrals.

Bridging

This section focuses on violence between couples. The comments and steps may be adapted to most domestic situations where there is violence.

Warning

- Do not try to do more than the essentials in the emergency. Refer for help for the underlying problems.
- *Beware* of situations where there is actual fighting. The participants will likely turn on you.

WHEN THERE IS CHILD SEXUAL ABUSE

Focus

a. Help the first aider to identify child abuse situations.
b. Develop skills in providing emotional first aid to individuals and families where there is child abuse. These include the abuser.
c. Become aware of legal responsibilities.

Illustrations

A. Wendy is eight. You are her school teacher. You have noticed that she has developed a fear of holidays and of going home after school. You have talked with her mother who reports that Wendy has been having nightmares, wakes up and is afraid of going back to sleep. Recently, there have been two absences from school. Wendy's father had written the excuses. Mother seemed surprised when you brought up the school absences.

B. Dorothy has invited you to her home because, "I have something important to talk over with you." She had been suspicious that her husband was involved sexually with their 15 year old daughter Susan. Dorothy and Susan had fought earlier in the day and Susan blurted out the family secret. Dad was in the background and heard it all. He left the house and hasn't returned. This is your first encounter with this kind of family situation. What do you do?

Comments

Child sexual abuse usually begins between 5-8 years of age and may well continue for a number of years before it is openly acknowledged by the family or is discovered by an outsider.

Society is becoming aware of the degree to which child sexual abuse is a problem. Available resources make it easier for the child and the non-offending parent to report incidents. As help becomes available for the offenders, they too have shown more readiness to get help.

The first aider needs to be concerned about both,
- the emotional trauma
- physical harm

The emotional damage will be different when the abuse has gone on for months and years than in first or second time situations. There will be more of an emotional storm in the new situations. The emotional storm may include a whole bunch of feelings for the child such as guilt, fear and shame.

The non-offending parent, usually the mother, will be experiencing another kind of emotional storm involving feelings of anger, inadequacy, remorse and fear of what the law will do to her spouse. There may also be feelings of relief, now that what she has "suspected" is out in the open.

If you are attempting to determine whether there is sexual abuse, the following behavior will provide clues. Several clues warrant investigation.

Pre-School Child

Fear of men
Return to baby-like behavior
Fear of the dark
Increased whinning and irritability

School Child

Illustration A combines several clues:
Nightmares
Loss of sleep
Fear of going home from school
Suspicious absences from school

Other clues to look for are:
Change in eating behavior, e.g. overeating
Physical symptoms such as abdominal pains or mouth bruises

Adolescent

Acting out, such as stealing, drugs or alcohol abuse
Turning to other families for nurture
Poor self-image
Keeping cool when talking about emotional experiences
Attempts at suicide

Step by Step Procedure

A. With the focus on *the child*.

1. Focus on establishing trust and ease with the child. You can do this by asking about friends and other normal conversation.
2. Make sure that the surroundings are comfortable, friendly and free of interruptions.
3. Try to get some idea of the child's needs and her stage of growing up. Do not use sexual terms which would be too mature.
4. Check your listening skills. See pp. 87.
5. Avoid questions that will put the child on guard. e.g. "Why did you...?"
6. Do not push the resistant child. Read the section on empathy, pp. 90.
7. Reassure the child with positive statements. e.g. "It helps a lot for you to tell me about this." "You will be okay and will not get punished." "Your father, grandfather, uncle (whoever is the offender) is the one who is responsible."
8. If the child's non-offending parent hasn't been informed or isn't present, tell the child that you have a duty to tell her mother.
9. If the child is old enough tell the child that you will be seeking help for the offender.

B. With the focus on the *non-offending parent*.

1. Establish trust. See the sections on listening, trust and empathy pp. 81-96.
2. Watch for your own feelings of anger, fear, etc. Avoid blame and showing shock.
3. Try to get a sense of whatever emotional storm she is experiencing.
4. Be positive in your statements. e.g. "It will help everybody involved now that you are talking about the situation."
5. Inform her where counselling is available. Encourage her to go to a professional for an assessment to determine whether therapy is indicated for herself, the child or the family.
6. Inform her that it is usual for the offender to get specialized help as well.
7. Tell her that you are bound legally to report the information to authorities. Different provinces or states may have different requirements and different places to report.
8. Offer your continued services as appropriate until some other helper has intervened.
9. Report as required by law.

C. With the focus on *the offender*.

1-4. Follow those for the non-offending parent immediately above. Be extremely cautious about your own anger and negative feelings. Instead, support his willingness to talk. e.g. "I'm glad that you can tell me about what's happened."

5. Confront the offender with the fact that he has a very serious problem and that in your opinion he needs special help. See the section on confronting pp. 126.

6. Tell him where he can get help. If you do not know where, you can do your checking together. Stick to your task until a referral has been made or another resource has intervened.

7. Tell him that what he is doing is against the law and that if you don't report it, you will be breaking the law.

8. Report to the appropriate authority. e.g. A mental health agency or professional. The appropriate provincial or state human resources agency.

Bridging The above material can be adapted to situations where there is physical abuse. See the section on physical abuse pp. 66.

Warning In meeting your legal obligations, do not go to the police except as a last resort or when your province requires direct reporting by you. Go to the appropriate agency instead and let them contact the police.

The issue is one of your gaining trust and not scaring the clients off and thus depriving them of the chance to get emotional first aid.

WHEN THERE IS BURNOUT

"Burnout" is a term used to describe emotional exhaustion experienced by some individuals who work as people helpers. It includes mental health workers, nurses, doctors, teachers, clergy.

Focus

a. Learn how to spot "burnout".
b. Know what steps to take to get the "burnout" victim to help him/herself.

Illustration

Claude works as a personnel officer in an unemployment centre. The government has cut back on funds for any additional staff while the number of unemployed have increased significantly.

The stress of the job has been draining for him. He feels exhausted. He has become very negative about his job and about himself. He has been drinking more than usual. Problems are escalating at home.

Comments

The term is used to describe the exhaustion and other emotional symptoms of people who are folding up as a result of intense involvement with the people they are helping. They may be professionals or para-professionals. They may be paid staff or volunteers.

The signs to watch for include the following:

- Negative feelings about oneself and one's ability to do his/her job well.
- Emotional exhaustion, feeling that "I can no longer give to my students."
- Cynical about the clients with whom I work. This includes hard and callous attitudes.
- Inappropriately leaving or threatening to leave one's job.
- Increased use of alcohol or drugs.
- Increase or emergence of problems at home.
- Ignoring the "burnout" signs.
- Sarcasm.
- Touchy and irritable.
- "I'll be retired in ten years, who cares anyway."
- "I'll just have to bite my upper lip and get on with it."

The intensity of these signs together with the frequency with which they occur determine whether or not it is an emergency.

If you suspect "burnout", do become familiar with the section on "When It's an Emergency" pp. 43 before you attempt to help the client in any particular way. It will help to listen until you know more clearly whether it's burnout.

If the signs are very intent and severe your client needs professional help! If things have escalated recently help is needed promptly! One of the important causes of burnout is the lack of a support system. Support systems can be used to prevent burnout. Also a good support group of peers is an excellent way of helping oneself when there is mild burnout and it's not an emergency.

First aiders do work that can lead to burnout for them. There is risk when providing emotional first aid is your full time job. There is risk when your other work is in helping people with problems, working with the sick, teaching, working as a priest or minister.

However, a group of peers is a superior route to go with mild burnout.

Step by Step Procedure

1. If you suspect burnout, use the burnout checklist of signs (in the Comments above).

2. If the signs are intense and happen frequently, it's likely severe burnout and should be treated as an emergency. See pp. 43.

3. The most important step in helping the client with severe burnout is to get him/her to go for professional help.

4. Professional pride may cause the client to resist going for help. See pp. 135 on how to handle resistance.

5. If the signs indicate mild burnout, (the symptoms are mild and do not occur frequently) encourage the client to get into a group of other professional helpers. S/he might start such a group.

6. With *mild* burnout, where the client understands what the problem is, you as first aider, may develop a helping relationship with the client. Together, you can follow through parts Two and Three of Chapter IV. The goal would be a change of work habits and/or in life style.

Bridging

This section will be more useful if the first aider also reads Chapter III, on When It's an Emergency pp. 41-78.

Warning

• Do not attempt to treat the severe burnout victim. Get professional help.

WHEN THERE IS DRUG INTOXICATION

Focus
a. Identify when drug intoxication is an emergency.
b. Learn what steps to take to help in the situation.

Illustration

The pastor of your local church calls you. He requests your help knowing that you are an emotional first aider. He directs you to a particular house where there is an emergency and you are expected. The emergency involves a mother and her 19 year old son. The son is spaced out on some drug. He is imagining all sorts of things. His eyes are glazed and he looks very pale. The mother is in a panic and is making a scene.

Comments

Usually the call for help will come from the family or from friends of the client. These calls to first aiders will be infrequent except in cases where the family or friends do not want to involve professionals and the authorities.

Most large centres will have detoxication units. However, some of these units will not be open on weekends or after five.

The client who is experiencing drug intoxication may be:
- Afraid of what is happening to his/her mind.
- Afraid of what is happening to his/her body.
- Out of touch with reality.
- Unconscious or feeling faint.
- In danger of harming others.
- In danger of self-harm.

The friend or family member who has called for help may be:
- Acutely anxious.
- Afraid for the client.
- Afraid of being hurt by the client.

It is important to remember that every drug intoxication situation is unique.

Do not argue with the client. S/he cannot reason. Get professional help for the client quickly. People die from drug intoxication.

Step by Step Procedure

1. Keep calm. Take time to assess the situation and to think about where to get professional help.
2. Provide life sustaining first aid. e.g. Place the client in a position so that s/he will not suffocate from vomit.
3. Send for professional help. e.g. Call an ambulance. You should already know where to find the telephone number of the detox centre.
4. Do whatever is necessary to prevent the situation from getting worse. e.g. Move the client to a safer place.
5. Attend to the anxiety of family and friends. See the section on Acute Anxiety pp. 55.
6. Be reassuring. Enlist the help of family and friends as they settle down.
7. Contact the client or family after the emergency and follow up with help. This may focus on encouraging the client to get professional help for the addiction.

Bridging

Two other sections have important information for you when faced with drug intoxication.
- The section on Working with the Alcoholic pp. 156.
- The section on When there is Acute Anxiety pp. 55.

Warning

During the follow up period *do not* attempt to provide support or counselling for the addict's emotional problems *unless* s/he is actively involved elsewhere in a treatment program for the addiction.

CHAPTER IV

HELPING PEOPLE WITH EMOTIONAL PROBLEMS

PART ONE

ACHIEVING A RELATIONSHIP

INTRODUCTION

This chapter covers the A B C's of helping people with emotional problems. It contains three parts. In Part One, "A" stands for **A**chieving the helping relationship and covers the early stages of the experience.[1]

In Part Two "B" stands for **B**oiling the problem down and covers that part of helping people to help themselves having to do with problem clarification and identification.

In Part Three "C" stands for **C**hallenging the client to cope and focuses on issues having to do with confronting and helping clients to take steps to resolve their problem(s).

The process of A B & C is explained in more detail in the section "Emotional First Aid as an Experience" pp 28. It would be helpful to read again the illustration in that section.

1   Jones, Warren L. — *The A-B-C Method of Crisis Management*; Mental Hygene (Jan. 1968), p. 87.

SKILLS NECESSARY FOR BUILDING THE HELPING RELATIONSHIP

This section is an introduction to the helping process with a focus on identifying skills necessary for establishing a helping relationship that works.

Focus

a. An understanding of how the helping process works when emotions are part of the problem.
b. Insight into the importance of the human need for adequate support systems in times of stress and crisis.
c. To identify various parts of the helping relationship.
d. To identify a list of skills necessary for an effective helping relationship.

Illustrations

A. The helper, a volunteer, and the client, a shipper in a warehouse, have met together once a week for three weeks. They had not met previously, but were introduced by the personnel manager of the company. Trust emerged quickly when the client was told that the helper would not be reporting back to the manager. They seemed to hit it off well, and for sessions number two and number three the client arrived ten minutes early. The employee had developed a lot of anxiety and had made some serious errors on the job. He was new to the city, having come six months ago from another province. He learned three months ago that his wife was not going to join him, that she has decided to end the marriage and is filing for custody of the children.

In the first meeting, he talked only of his fear of losing his job and the mistakes he had made. In the second and third sessions he talked freely of his family and marital situation and of his loneliness in his new apartment.

B. Janice was introduced to the helper through her church. They had a couple of hours together for their first visit which took place in the lounge of the church. She came away feeling that the helper had talked down to her and that they were not meeting as equals. She also had a feeling that the helper would talk to other people in the church. She had no evidence for the mistrust except that there was no reassurance that the discussion between them was confidential. Janice did not go back for another meeting.

Comments
In situation A, a good relationship developed quickly. The helper in situation B made two mistakes and lost the client.

It takes both skill and time to achieve a creative helping alliance or relationship. It is very common for the helper to come in with a lot of questions at the beginning, motivated by curiosity about the problem and the helper's own desire to offer and provide a ready solution to the problem.

Most hurting people will avoid and withdraw from such questioning, feeling violated, or misunderstood and uncared for. Even the dependent, impatient individuals who demand a ready solution will usually back off from such questions feeling that your solution isn't any good. They will fall back to their own tried and found-to-be-wanting patterns of solving their problem.

Step by Step Procedure

1. Recall some time in your own experience when you were under stress in a complicated problem situation. Get into the situation by recalling the physical setting and some of the people in your life at that time.

2. a) which relationships were helpful to you in:
   i) sharing your emotions?
   ii) finding solutions to your problem?
   b) which relationships were not helpful in each of these areas?

3. Make a list of the factors in those helping relationships which were positive for you.

4. Discuss your list with another person.

5. Compare your joint lists with the following list which includes:
   Trust
   Empathy
   Acceptance
   Some real sense of partnership and equality and not being talked down to
   Encouragement to work out your own solution with support from the helper
   Limited advice-giving
   Very few questions
   A feeling of confidence in the helper.

6. Check the list below and select the skills you want to develop.
   The first part of this chapter provides ideas for you to develop skills in achieving a creative, helping relationship. Some of the important elements in such a relationship are as follows:
   - Information is listened to.
   - Feelings are listened to and understood.
   - There is empathy.
   - There is trust.
   - There is acceptance.
   - The contract or covenant is clear.
   - There is an appropriate level of inter-dependence (working together).

Bridging   The idea of a two-way working relationship or alliance applies to other situations such as the following:

☆ A parent and child learning how to play a new game or to put together a model plane.

☆ A couple touring a new country, and one of them had been there before.

☆ The author of this book and the helper who is reading the material and is encouraged to contact the writer for clarification and with suggestions for improving the book.

In each of these situations there are three common factors.

● Both parties are learning together while one has more experience in the field.

● An element of trust becomes necessary for the relationship to continue and to be productive.

● A team relationship develops and the relationship becomes the major factor in the learning and growth of the less experienced partner.

Warning   This particular step by step procedure is not to be used with clients. It is a learning tool aimed at improving the first aider's understanding of the helping relationship. The step by step procedures in most of the other sections are for use with clients.

Client nurturing the helper. What went wrong?

LISTENING SKILLS

Focus
  a. The helper is having difficulty in listening to the helpee. "I do all the talking. I can't remember what was communicated to me."
  b. The need to be able to distinguish between listening for verbal and for non-verbal information.
  c. The need to be able to listen for feelings.
  d. The need to be aware of one's own feelings and emotions.
  e. Practicing various listening skills with another helper.
  f. Evaluating one's ability to use effective listening skills.

Illustration

The 25 year old woman I'm trying to help just sits looking sad and only talks in very short responses to my questions. I keep asking questions until I run out of ideas and get very little in return.

I'm so used to the question and answer method (learned it in school) that I don't seem to have other ways of relating to this new person. I want information so I can understand her problem. I've met with her twice and don't know her any better than at the very first.

Comments

In the illustration, the first aider is doing too much of the work and too little listening. Listening in a helpful way is one of the most difficult skills helpers need to learn. Listening involves the skill of making oneself available to an individual, a couple, family or a small group (committee). Creative listening enables the helper to hear and observe
- information which is accurate
- clues or symbols which provide information
- feelings which inform the helper about the feeling side of the person's hurts, joys
- non-verbal information which is communicated by gestures, eye movements, body position, etc.

Effective listening is more than getting information and feelings. Effective listening in itself is helpful to the client, for if we listen well, the client
- feels understood;
- feels cared about;
- is helped to develop trust in the helper;
- is helped through the talking process to unload pent up feelings;

- is helped through the talking process to clarify his/her problem;
- is helped toward self-discovery and self-understanding.

The simple act of listening, as most people know it, must be distinguished from "active listening." Active listening includes the notion of some response by me which makes it easier for the client to continue to share more information and feelings.

In our eagerness to get information, we often resort to asking questions, or to do all the talking ourselves. When we do this, the client does not get the opportunities and benefits described above. In fact, an early blunt personal question usually serves to lower trust, or even to violate the client who then becomes scared and shuts down further. The client may give the information and shut down later, or just disappear. Often silence, instead of questions, is very helpful for the relationship. However, letting silence happen is not easy for some first aiders.

It is helpful to develop listening skills which enable us to understand the client, to remember what was communicated without taking notes and show we really care. It is not easy to be listening for information and feelings and to be making the appropriate verbal and/or non-verbal responses all at the same time. Not all help is helpful and the ability to listen effectively has a lot to do with the quality of help given and whether the helping relationship gets off the ground.

Most of us have to work on keeping our biases, prejudices, value judgments and experiences out of the way so we can hear what is being communicated. We tend to hear what we want to hear and screen out what we don't want to hear. We also tend to understand the client's experiences only through our own experiences. In the process of translation, the message or information gets changed into something different than what the client actually experienced. The result is that the client ends up feeling misunderstood and lonely.

Thinking about solutions instead of listening

Step by Step Procedure

1. Decide at the beginning not to ask any questions which allow a "yes" or a "no". Instead, inquire in ways which encourage the client to offer information and to tell his/her story.

2. When you find yourself about to ask a specific question, think about how you can word your statement so that it becomes an invitation for the client to share. You are wondering whether the new person you're helping has any children. You can ask: "Do you have any children?" or you can offer an invitation: "I'm interested in your family, and would like you to tell me as much as you like about the family and maybe how they are connected to your problem."

3. Concentrate first on listening for information separately from listening for feelings. For another portion of the time together, concentrate on listening for feelings instead of factual information.

4. After you have developed some skills in listening for information and feelings, then concentrate on listening for both at the same time.

5. Keep your responses down to a minimum.

6. After you have mastered Step 4, focus on listening more for non-verbal communication. Make your list of as many non-verbal things to watch for as you can think of. These should include at least the following:

How people hold their body	Silence
Heavy or light breathing	Tears
Sighs	Eye movement
Relaxed or tense, etc.	Eye contact
Hand gestures	Facial expressions

7. Observe symbols which communicate both information and feelings. Take time to be aware of what the client may be communicating by the kinds of clothes worn, jewellery, make-up, hair style, house, car, etc. Try to formulate some ideas about what these mean without asking questions, passing judgement or letting your bias get in the way of your understanding. e.g. If you don't like long hair, don't let your bias block or distort the message in the symbol.

8. Take time to fit all the information you have obtained into your understanding of the whole person you're helping. Do not attempt to communicate any overall picture back to the client at this point.

9. Right after the session together, check out to what extent during the meeting you:
   a) permitted outside noises, happenings or interruptions to distract your focus on the client and his/her situation;
   b) allowed your thoughts to run to similar experiences or problems you have had;
   c) started forming thoughts about what the problem is, or what kind of person this is before you have a lot of relevant information.

10. Make mental notes to avoid doing a., b. and c. above in the next meeting with a client. Keep your attention on the person(s) so that trust and feelings of being understood develop.

Bridging Involved in the example above are a number of related problems.
- The need to build trust prior to getting information of a factual nature.
- We seem to be avoiding contact and further times together.
- The client only wants to talk about my situation.
- The client seems to be loaded with feelings and I don't know how to make it easy for her to unload.
- I'm aware that asking questions may be related to some of my own anxiety.
- I may be asking a lot of questions related to a) my own past experiences and b) hunches I'm making about her problems.
- I ask questions and get nothing but yes or no.

Warning ☆ 1. As you gain skills in hearing information and feelings, you may pick up some things which scare you. e.g. a threat of suicide, or anger which may lead to violence. Keep calm, communicate acceptance and be firm in bringing some other person into the situation who can deal with the more serious stuff. That person would most often be a professional like a medical doctor, pastoral counselor, hospital chaplain or mental health worker.

☆ 2. Do not avoid asking for help from professionals because you do not know how to keep confidences. You can learn ways to talk about cases without betraying confidentiality. (See the section on confidentiality, pp. 159).

This client feels understood

DEVELOPING EMPATHY

Focus

  a. Establish a positive helping relationship early in the volunteer situation.

  b. Increase one's understanding of what is really going on with the client.

  c. Avoid getting one's own problems mixed up with the client's problems. The client's problems are already complex.

Illustration

A 47 year old man with two teenage sons recently lost his wife in an accident. At the end of two meetings with him he seems distant and is giving you a message which seems to say "You don't understand." You've asked him all sorts of questions about his situation and even told him about the death of your mother some ten years earlier. These efforts to develop empathy are not working for you.

Comments

Involved in this example are several related concerns. These include:

● The need for the client to feel that s/he is not alone with his problem.

● That there is someone who understands his pain, loss and confusion.

● The client's need for self-reassurance that he is not going crazy and is capable of revealing what he is really thinking and feeling.

A premature effort at resolving a problem results in failure largely because the client is unclear about the problem and its various parts. Further, intense emotions contribute to the confusion.

In troubled times, people tend to feel lonelier than usual. In addition, their support system is often too small. This may have contributed to the problem in the first place.

The helper sometimes gets emotionally involved in the client's problem:

● tends to lose sleep.

● thinks a lot about the client and finds him/herself either avoiding the client or wanting to make inappropriate contact.

● gets too anxious.

Empathy is the ability to put oneself in another person's shoes, to get into his/her way of experiencing feelings about the situation and understanding the problem. It means keeping one's head clear about the real world from which you come as a helper and at the same time getting into the client's shoes, without becoming part of the problem. Empathy is one of the most useful qualities (skills) that a helper can bring to troubled people. It is not the same as sympathy.

Sympathy is sharing another's feelings and experiences even to the extent of feeling sorry for them. An example would be when a friend's spouse dies and you go to the home the same day and fully experience the immediate grief with him/her. You become one more person going through and experiencing the grief.

While sympathy can be helpful in grief situations, however, it does not help the individual to feel good enough about him/herself to tackle the situation and work through it for himself. Some people feel smothered by sympathy. Others think you feel sorry for them, then they feel inferior to you.

Do not attempt to develop total empathy. Feeling understood, accepted and cared for does not require being totally understood. It's scary for some people to give another person the power of totally understanding them, their feelings and inner thoughts.

Sometimes in our eagerness to let the other person know we understand, we tell them about our own similar experiences. This usually conveys the message that we don't care about them and their problem. When emotions are heavy, the emotions add to the confused state of the client. Clients cool down and become clear by retelling their story. We do need to let people know we understand and care. However, there are better ways of doing this than by telling our story. e.g. Active listening, keeping appointments, maintaining trust and confidentiality.

When people feel that they are understood they are more likely to remain in the helper-client relationship as long as necessary instead of terminating inappropriately.

Step by Step
Procedure 1. Decide at the beginning that you will not tell your similar story, no matter how much you think about it. Decide instead to pay full attention to the client.

2. Attend by listening as outlined on pp. 85.

3. Attend by not allowing anything outside to distract you from being with the person. Try to maintain the amount of eye contact the client is comfortable with.

4. If you come to a clear understanding of the client's feelings or the problem situation communicate your understanding by a) saying "I'm beginning to understand" or b) by a simple touch on the arm if it seems appropriate. Show that you are wanting to understand by suggesting that the client "Go over that again" or "Tell me what you are feeling in a little different way, so I can understand."

5. Check out your own feeling responses as you listen.

6. Acknowledge to yourself any feelings you are having, but don't act on them during the session. If you need to talk to another person about your own feeling responses or emotional involvement in your client's problem, share this confidentially with another helper at a later time.

7. Practice developing empathy skills as you listen to your children or your friends; it's a universal skill!

Bridging   Developing empathy is an excellent way to improve the quality of any meaningful relationship. Try these skills with your family and close friends. Your work relationship may offer you another opportunity.

Warning   If you find that being empathic wears you out and emotionally drains you, it could be 1) that you are into sympathy and not empathy, or 2) that the problem is too close to some of your own unresolved emotions. You should either discontinue the relationship by referring the client to a professional or another first aider and/or talk to a professional about what is happening to you. See the section "The Helper Gets Help".

DEVELOPING TRUST

Focus

a. The helper senses that the client doesn't trust him/her.
b. The helper asks a lot of questions but the client is reluctant to give any information.
c. The client was sent to me or was told that s/he had to get help "or else."
d. The helper is caught in a triangle with the client, one of his/her family members or a boss or supervisor.
e. The client is convinced that my experiences and life style are so different from his or hers, that I could not possibly understand.

Illustrations

A. The client has been told that he will be dismissed from his job in two months if he doesn't get help for his drinking. He has come to you for help. You are in the employ of the same company and have connections with his supervisor.

B. The client has been sent to you by her spouse because she is depressed and her husband is threatening to leave the marriage. You are social friends with both of these people. You are aware that she doesn't think that she has a problem and that her husband just doesn't want to be around home anymore.

Comments

In both of the illustrations, the client's motivation to get help or to help him/herself is in question. What you do to help build trust will have a major impact on whether the helping relationship will work. Both of the illustrations involve a triangle where trust will be at a low ebb.

Trust building will be difficult where the helper does not listen well. It will be almost impossible if the client has reason to suspect that what he shares is not confidential and private.

Trust building can be difficult if there are wide differences between the helper and the client; socially, academically, culturally, language-wise or age-wise.

Sometimes the client thinks that his experiences are so weird or feels that s/he has been so bad, that he cannot believe that the helper will understand.

Developing Trust

The illustrations point to situations where some mistrust would be normal. This will grow if not attended to. Developing trust is essential from the very beginning of a meeting. Trust building requires skills in both empathy and listening. There are a number of simple and practical, but sometimes difficult, lessons to learn about building trust.

The most important element in trust building is for the helper to be trustworthy. It is important to promise only what one has the time, ability and motivation to provide. For example, it would not be fair to make a promise to someone that you would never let them down, then forget to show up in time for your next meeting.

Be fully aware of your limitations, and be honest in not offering help that is not clearly within these limitations. There are limitations of time, distance and your own skills. Beware; your own need to help and nurture may trick you into promising more than you can offer!

The client will not trust you if you tell him or her one little bit of gossip or confidential information about someone else. S/he is correct in assuming that if you tell on others, you will also talk to others about him/her. It is usually helpful and most important to establish very early in the first meeting that what s/he shares with you is confidential and that it will not be repeated elsewhere without his/her permission.

There are helpful ways for building trust when the client feels that his solution is weird or bad. Some helpers think that they need to share similar experiences as a way of getting the client to trust. This method has serious drawbacks and can easily destroy what little trust may have developed. It is much safer and more effective to use empathy and listening skills. You can respond to feelings without telling your own or someone else's story. You can tell the client that you are trying to understand and encourage him/her to tell you more or to "go over that again."

Above all it is important that you avoid two common errors. 1) That of being critical and judgmental and 2) showing shock or disbelief.

The ideas and warnings in the preceding paragraphs apply as well to situations where there are cultural, social, age, academic or economic gaps between you and the client. If you are not prepared to take steps to get informed about and to develop some understanding for the other person's life style it would be better to discontinue the helping relationship and to make a good referral.

Step by Step Procedure

1. When you first notice that trust is an issue, at the beginning of a meeting you could comment on the situation such as: "It's not easy to open oneself to help in a new situation such as we find ourselves now" or, "It's usually difficult to get down to what hurts or troubles us when we are not sure what the other person will do with what is revealed." If it's a triangle situation you can comment, "Each of us is aware of the potential problem of our both working for the same company, maybe we could talk a bit about confidentiality and private information."

2. Use your best listening and empathy skills and let the client know that you care about his feelings and pain more than the story he is telling.

3. Communicate messages of acceptance (and not criticism) without approving of his behavior or mistakes.

4. Listen for any unrealistic expectations and clearly state in a positive way your limits of time and ability to help. Clearly state what you expect and are offering by way of help.

5. Check out the client's response to what you offer, hear his/her expectation and be frank about what you can or cannot do.

6. Check out your own feeling responses to whatever may have sounded "weird" or "bad" in the client's story or the way he acted. Make a mental note to check out any strong reactions with a peer or consultant following your session, before you get together with your client again. (See the section on confidentiality, pp. 159).

7. Before the meeting ends, make certain that both you and the client are absolutely clear about any contracts, agreements made between you. e.g. (when you will meet again, matters of confidentiality, who has promised to do what and when.) Offer to be available in between meetings only:
   - if the client expects to be in an emergency and
   - if you are certain that you can be available and can produce.

8. As the meeting draws to a close, communicate to the client that you appreciate the risk s/he took in sharing herself/himself with you and that you will be looking forward to your next meeting.

Bridging   This material on trust applies to other situations such as:
- Parenting children
- Friendships
- As a supervisor at work
- Most professional and business relationships.

Warning   There are some individuals (first type) who, by character, are extremely suspicious and who will not be able to respond with trust to any of your best skills. Other rather normal people (second type) under extreme stress may develop, for a brief period, a suspicious or paranoid state.

It is important that you learn some of the major clues for identifying which type of paranoia (suspiciousness) you are facing in a client. Most paranoid persons are not dangerous to the helper; however, you will be wasting your time trying to develop a helping relationship with the first type and you will do the second type a disservice if you write him/her off without using your very best trust building skills.

These folk require a great amount of trustworthiness from their helper. You will be important to them and you also will require supervision or consultation from an expert in order not to get caught in their suspicions and lose the helping relationship. Ordinary empathy and listening skills will not likely work with either of the above.

There is an excellent chapter on the "Paranoid" in a book by Eugene Kennedy "On Becoming a Counselor".[1]

1   Kennedy, Eugene; *On Becoming a Counselor*, 1977
     Seabury Press, New York.

ESTABLISHING THE CONTRACT OR COVENANT

The contract or covenant needs special attention because it has to do with expectations on the part of both helper and client. The expectations are there anyway whether or not there is any clear understanding about a covenant or contract. Agreements about times, who will be doing what and what the helping relationship is about and what it is supposed to accomplish are parts of the contract. A contract also has to do with commitment, promises and the caring which gets connected to these commitments.

Focus

a. Both the helper and the client are having difficulty in maintaining regular times for meeting. It is usually hit and miss.

b. Meetings end and it is not clear as to what happens next or when the next meeting will be.

c. The helper is not clear as to why s/he is working with this particular client.

d. The client appears to be expecting 1) some things which were not in the original agreement or 2) things or help from the helper which he is not prepared or able to give.

e. The helper feels manipulated by the client and there is no clear contract to fall back on.

f. The helper is caught in uncomfortable self-defense or self-protection.

Illustrations

A. The helper has had three meetings with Jim over three weeks. Jim has been very anxious and down about the break-up with his fiancee. He is operating with considerable confusion about a lot of things and this is affecting his work. After each meeting one of you has to make a phone call about the next meeting. The helper got his days confused one week and it appears that the helper has picked up some of Jim's confusion.

B. The client has picked up somehow that the helper would be taking her to dinner either in her home or to a restaurant. The helper was surprised and wondered whether she had inadvertently implied that she would like to do this or whether it was sheer fantasy on the part of the client. It could be that the client is simply depressed, lonely and clinging; yet it is not appropriate nor do you care to take her to dinner.

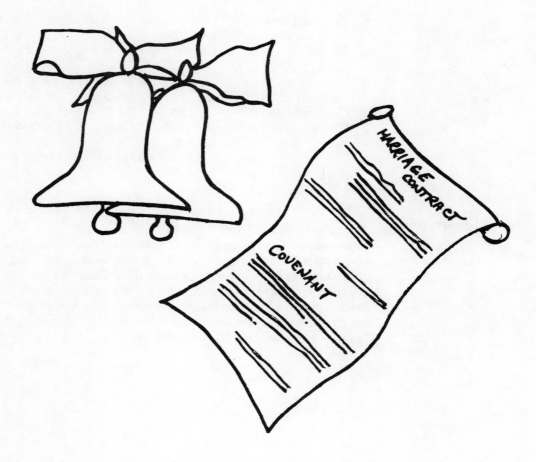

Keep contracts clean and simple

Comments   In the illustrations, problems developed because contracts were not clear. The more persons there are in the helping situation, the greater is the need for a clear and simple contract.

Likewise, the greater the stress and/or confusion being experienced by the client, the greater is the need to establish a clear and simple contract.

Clients and helpers always have their expectations, regardless of whether or not those expectations are verbalized or clarified. There are those expectations that each bring to the helping relationship and there are those expectations which emerge during the meeting and sometimes during the interval between meetings.

It is common for the helper to assume that the client is capable of being as clear about expectations and contracts as the average person who is without stress. This often leads to frustrations with the client and sometimes to outright blaming and fault finding. The client assumes something is wrong, misunderstands the arrangements or gets times mixed up.

Taking time to get the client to clarify and put out his/ her expectations promotes the health of the client and aids in his/her skills for problem solving.

Having the experience of making clear agreements with the helper and keeping those agreements also leads to good health and life enriching skills. It provides the client with security while going through a stressful time. For some clients, it is one of the first relationships which is clear in its boundaries and expectations.

Step by Step Procedure

1. As soon as there is some relationship established, inquire of the client just what s/he understands about why you are meeting.
2. Summarize your understanding of the meeting at the same time reporting who did what to bring you together.
3. After there has been considerable opportunity to establish some helping relationship and toward the end of the first meeting, have the client spell out his/her expectations of what is going to take place in future meetings and what is expected by way of help.
4. Then be clear in putting out your own expectations about what you are able and not able to do, about time available and how often you will meet and/or talk to one another.
5. Be very clear about the following. Where the next meeting takes place. Obligations such as fees, taking steps to do specific things e.g. an alcoholic getting into AA. Whether you will be reporting the new contract to any other counsellor or therapist working with the client.
6. After three or four meetings, be sure to clarify each other's expectations. They may still be unclear or may have changed.
7. If you are picking up anything which sounds like expectations which you have not agreed to, act now and talk to the client about it.
8. Always be clear with each other at the end of a meeting about the agreements around the next time and place of meeting.
9. Remember, a contract about what will happen and when should be developed with every client.

Bridging

The ideas and steps suggested here for establishing a contract or covenant with the client apply to working with individuals, couples, families, workshops or teaching groups. The ideas and steps also apply to planning in staff groups or anywhere you are providing leadership.

Warning

There are two traps to watch for in the area of contracting.
- There is the danger of paying so much attention to contracting that one neglects empathy, caring and acceptance.
- There is the danger of working so hard at warmth, caring and empathy that the whole helping relationship breaks down because of the confusion of expectations. In the long run, it is easier to be caring, warm and accepting when contracts and expectations are clearly understood.

DEPENDENCY ISSUES

Feelings and attitudes about being dependent or independent are often counter-productive in helping relationships. In this section, we will give attention to dependency issues for both the helper and the client. To begin with, the concepts, dependent, independent and interdependent may be confusing for you. Read the whole section carefully.

Dependency in providing emotional first aid has to do with three areas:

- Fostering appropriate dependent and independent behavior while helping people to help themselves.
- Responding to the feelings and fears the client may have about his/her dependent needs, often strong enough to make it almost impossible to ask for or to go for help.
- Understanding one's own feelings and attitudes about being dependent or about having others dependent on us for help.

Focus

a. The client is giving clear messages that s/he wants a quick and easy answer/solution to the problem. The client expects the helper to give advice or even to solve the problem for him/her.

b. The client keeps talking about ending the meetings and insisting that things are better and s/he can do the rest on her/ his own.

c. The client is asking for help for the first time in years, is a self-made person and believes that personal and emotional problems should be kept to and resolved by oneself. S/he may believe "if you just give things time, the problem will resolve itself."

d. The client is the clinging dependent type, wants extra time, doesn't have many friends, and even follows the helper about the room.

e. The helper has been meeting with this client for many months and would like to terminate. She is uncomfortable with the client's dependency needs. e.g. That the client depends upon her for advice, friendship, etc.

Illustration   A young man of twenty-one is still living with his parents and struggling with dependency conflicts. e.g. He looks for support from his parents but gets angry, telling them to get off his back, whenever they offer him sound advice.

He is being seen because his drinking is interferring with his work. He likes his work and has been productive. He gets along well with the other employees. He wants very much to save his job. However, he insists that he can get things under control without your help or the help of AA. At the end of each of the first three sessions, he said he wasn't coming back. Yet in between he calls and wants to talk to you again. Usually he avoids discussion about the hangovers and the absenteeism. This client is wavering back and forth between wanting to be dependent and resisting help because he is afraid of becoming dependent.

Comments   One of the basic helping principles, 'that of helping people to help themselves' implies that there is an *appropriate* dependency in the helping situation and that the help need not be destructive or damaging to the client through taking away his sense of self-worth and independence.

A look at the course of the dependency struggle from birth to maturity will help us to understand how dependency may be at work in a helping relationship. We are born totally dependent on others. Maturity involves being interdependent with others at appropriate times and in appropriate ways. Receiving and learning from others; giving to and helping others as a matter of course in daily living. Along the way to this maturity and inter-dependence, the child struggles with his/her dependency conflicts from age two onward through the teens. The teenager will rebel when the parents refuse the car on a particular night, and yet feels secretly grateful for the "no" because she fears that there will be drinking in the car. The dependency conflict is in full bloom.

Quite capable, independent adults will sometimes show similar conflict during an emotional crisis. Too often in our individualistic society, there is a tendency to stay away from help for emotional crises for fear of being seen as dependent, weak or sick.

Newly trained counsellors and helpers tend to avoid getting supervision or help with a troublesome situation or with feelings of burn out and fatigue, because of their fear of being seen as weak.

The client may settle into a helping relationship where appropriate dependency is evident. As the client moves toward better emotional health, considerable independence may be expressed. Like the teenager, the client needs to express independence as part of becoming inter-dependent with his/her support system.

Step by Step
Procedure 1.   In any new helping situation, it is important to try to gauge where the client is with regard to his dependency feelings toward you and the helping situation. Try to gauge this by how the client goes about asking for help, by things the client says, by mannerisms and expectations. The average depressed client may begin by being very dependent. A compulsive somewhat anxious super performer may be quite independent.

2.   In either case, respond to the dependency by accepting the client where s/he is and communicate that it is okay to feel that way just now.

3. As trust develops, gradually explain to the independent client that one of the reasons s/he has been having such difficulty with emotions and/or problems may be the result of trying too hard to work through things alone. Explain that this is an area of life where self-reliance can be a handicap. While communicating this material, be sure to support any stoic approach to life which the client values. A stoic approach to life, which includes appropriate dependency, is to be highly valued.

4. Very early in the helping relationship, communicate to the dependent client that you are available as contracted, that you will provide emotional support; that you cannot do his work for him/her and that you do not have any magic solutions.

5. As the relationship develops, from time to time check out with your clients how they see and feel about the dependent side of the relationship. Give the client encouragement around any moves made toward more appropriate dependency behavior.

6. Check out your own feelings about having a client dependent upon you.

7. Check out whether or not you have need for clients to be dependent on you in inappropriate ways and amounts.

8. Check out whether you feel free to turn to a supervisor or mental health consultant seeking help for working with the client.

Bridging   The comments in this session about dependency, its conflicts and its appropriateness may also apply to the helper in relation to getting supervision, using consultation or to referring clients to other helpers.

Warning   • Some of the above steps do not apply to people who need an unusual amount of dependency just to function in their job or in life.
   • Supportive counselling may include a lot of dependency on the part of a client who is retarded or just out after many years in the hospital. The principle of 'helping people to help themselves' still applies in the supportive relationship. See Chapter V for additional reading (pp. 145).
   • Giving information may be different than offering advice to the dependent client. It is important to make the distinction. Giving information which is not being requested or which the client could easily obtain by going to the library or to his/ her bank, may be detrimental to growth and health.

CHAPTER IV

PART TWO

BOILING THE PROBLEM DOWN

INTRODUCTION

Focus

a. Understanding the relationship between emotions, support systems and problem identification/clarification.
b. Understanding the role of the helper in boiling the problem down.
c. Identifying a list of skills necessary for effectively helping a client with problem identification and clarification.

Illustrations

A. *A situation which is going well.*

Alice is a 45 year old single parent. Her son, 23 and daughter 20 are both about to move out. Recently she has become very anxious. This is your third meeting with her. Talking with you has helped her to calm down. In this third session she has cried less and you are helping her to talk in a coherent way about such things as how she has always had people around her at home, how she has depended on family for her social life; etc, how much she has enjoyed her job and the people she has met through the job, and about her part in the up-coming wedding of her son, which she approves. The various parts of her problem are becoming clearer to you.

B. *A situation where confusion is widespread in spite of all your efforts at clarification.*

Jim is 62 and has worked for the same company for 20 years. His foreman has noticed recently that the quality of his work has slipped and that Jim seems depressed. The helping relationship appears to be well established and he has been on time for each meeting. This is the third session. He has talked about several problems he has at work and in his home life. Your efforts have been to pick up on any problem which appears important to him and to try to explain to him what is likely depressing him. Both of you are getting more and more confused as the meeting nears its end.

Comments

In illustration A above, the client is being helped to identify and clarify her problem. In situation B, both the client and the helper are bogged down because the first aider is not equipped to help with problem clarification.

Using our model of helping people to help themselves requires among other skills:

- knowledge of how to identify and clarify problems.
- a commitment to helping the client to identify and clarify the problem without doing the work for the client.
- being able to know quickly what the client needs, yet having the ability to *keep your ideas to yourself*, while helping the client to do his/her own clarification.

Occasionally in emergencies, you will need to come to your own conclusions. If the problem is confusing for you, talk things over with another skilled person, providing there is time.

You will then need to inform the client of your conclusions about the problem and what actions you plan to take.

Emergencies exist when the client is not capable of protecting him/herself, or when other persons have to be protected from the client.

You do not need to be totally clear about the client's problem(s) when you refer to a professional. It does help if you are clear about why you are referring.

For most first aiders, it's easier to come to your own conclusions about the client's problem than it is to be the one who aids the client in identifying and clarifying the problem for him/herself.

**Step by Step
Procedure**

1. Recall having watched a small child of three working on a toy workbench or similar toy where problem solving is involved. Note the child's need to find out for him/herself. Note also
    the different ways in which the parent was helpful; also ways which were not helpful to the child.

2. Recall a time in your own life when you were faced with a major problem which was stressful for you and which got resolved.
    - Note how you went about clarifying your problem.
        - i) what information you got.
        - ii) where you got the information.
        - iii) with whom you shared your problem.
    - Make a list of who was helpful and who was not.
    - Recall how much you did for yourself in the experience and list your points.
    - Try to distinguish between getting information and being given advice re: how to solve your problem.

3. Share your lists and findings with another person and make a joint list of skills necessary in helping a client with problem clarification.

4. Compare your joint list with my list which includes:
    - ☆ Being genuinely curious about the client's problem. Asking for clarification.
    - ☆ Accepting the client's confusion and sharing your own difficulty in understanding.
    - ☆ Helping the client to focus on identifiable parts of the problem.
    - ☆ Helping the client to understand who owns the various parts of the problem.
    - ☆ Helping the client when past experiences or strong emotional feelings may be distorting his/her understanding of the problem.
    - ☆ Encouraging the client to get more accurate information thus leading to clarity about reality.
    - ☆ Encouraging the client to tell you about the problem from a different perspective or point of view.
    - ☆ Helping the client to understand that his/her usual response to a stressful problem eg. drinking, is an ineffective effort at solving the problem.

Bridging   The material in this section may be useful wherever, problem solving is involved, such as teaching, parenting or supervision.

Warning   This session is an introduction to identifying and learning the skills necessary in helping a client with problem identification and clarification.
     These step by step procedures are not for use with clients, as they are in most other sections.

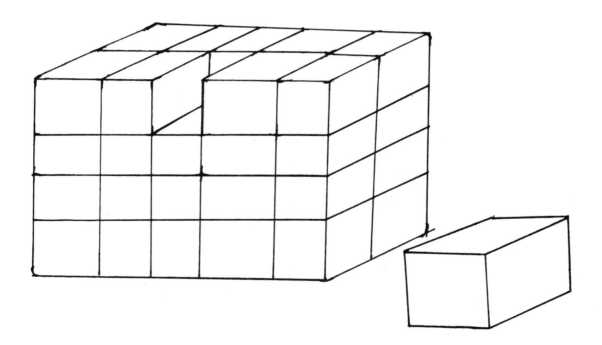

HELPING A CLIENT TO IDENTIFY A PROBLEM

Focus

a. Appropriate timing to begin helping the client with problem identification and clarification.
b. The ability to distinguish between the easier tasks of getting information and the tasks of helping with problem identification.
c. To identify patterns, games or defenses the client may be using to avoid looking at or owning the problem.
d. Specific skills which facilitate problem identification.

Illustration

Bill is a volunteer first aider with a crisis centre. At work, he is a trouble shooter with a regional computer sales firm where he focuses on getting new equipment running smoothly. He's not doing too well as a first aider. Clients feel that Bill has a lot of solutions to their problems which don't work. In the first meeting, Bill tends to go after information and immediately to begin working on the client's solution.

The client claims that Bill's not realistic and that he doesn't understand. The client does not return for further meetings.

Comments

There are a number of factors which make it difficult for clients to identify their problems. One or more of the following factors may be at work.

- The intensity of the emotions leave the client confused and often take so much energy that there is none left for clear thinking. The intensity of the emotions may lead the client to think that s/he is going crazy and will lose control. The resulting fear increases the emotional load.
- The pressures which are external to the client's emotional system may be coming from various sources and the client may feel bombarded and unable to focus on any one of those pressures.

Blaming avoids facing oneself

- One common factor when under stress is to blame others. This 'blaming' distorts and denies one's own part in the problem and results in spending one's energy in the wrong place and in futile efforts.
- The client's part in creating the problem may be so scary to the client that s/he finds it almost impossible to look at that scary stuff. This is particularly the case where anger, denial or guilt feelings are part of the client's problem.
- The client may be attempting to solve or deny the problem through the use of alcohol or drugs. This creates further confusion and inability to identify the problem.
- The client may have very few problem solving skills and some training may be helpful. However, unless the emotional aspects of the problem are attended to, most of the usual problem identification skills taught in industry or organizations will not work. Having attended to the emotional load and the client's patterns of responding to stress (e.g. denying, blaming) then the usual problem identification skills will be helpful.

Step by Step Procedure

1. Check your sense of whether the helping relationship is established sufficiently to allow you and the client to move into problem identification and clarification. Is there trust? Is there a contract? Does the client feel that you understand him/her?

2. Note whether the client has settled down, is less depressed and is ready to work on problem identification and his/her part in the problem. You may be right in thinking that it's the problem(s) which is causing the anxiety, confusion or depression. Hence you may feel an urge to get on with getting rid of the cause. However, your impatience may become a major obstacle and good timing is critical. Too much haste could guarantee failure, increased anxiety or depression. On the other hand, wallowing around and avoiding the problem for too long could mean that you, the helper, become part of the client's methods of avoiding the problem.

3. Assuming the time is now, begin to move toward problem identification with some reference to problems talked about. Express your need to be clearer about just what the problem is. e.g. "You've talked about a number of things which are upsetting you. I'm curious and feel a need to be clearer myself about the problem and what's at the root of it. I wonder if we could begin exploring it together." As part of this step, you might try some of the following depending on the client's confusion and tendency to avoid the problem.
   - Ask the client to put himself in the shoes of some more objective person in the family or network and to tell you about the problem from where that person sits. e.g. What do you think your brother would say is the problem.
   - Encourage the client to try to identify what feelings emerge or what usual patterns of behavior take place whenever she thinks much about the problem.

4. Suggest to the client that one reason s/he is caught in the problem is because he has failed to look at the problem from other angles. Encourage the client to move from vague to specific descriptions of the problem or its parts.

5. When the client continues to be vague or is bringing up several unrelated issues "like blaming someone else", use a technique like, "I'm still not very clear about what the problem is; let's run through it again."

Bridging   Although the suggested steps and illustrations in this section focus on helping an individual, couple or family, much of the material in this section is useful in other settings.

☆ It can be used by the helpers in working on their own confusion, anxiety about a problem or as a beginning toward finding a solution to a personal or work problem. This applies to situations where you are the helper and are confused or anxious about the situation.

☆ The theory and practical skills are useful in working with groups.

☆ The material can be used when applied to improving productivity and atmosphere in an organization or corporation.

☆ It can be used by parents, teachers and supervisors.

Warning   When a client is confused and extremely emotional, *do not pressure* the client to identify his/her problem. Be gentle and supportive. Watch out for your own low tolerance for not knowing what the problem is.

HELPING A CLIENT TO CLARIFY A PROBLEM

Focus

a. How to be helpful to a client in clarifying the problem by identifying its various parts.
b. How to help by identifying who owns the problem and parts of the problem.
c. How to help the client understand which parts of the problem may be open to resolution and which parts are not resolvable now and may be beyond any power which the client possesses.

Illustration

Elmer knows that his problem is his unhappiness in his marriage and in particular that he has been disappointed from the beginning because his wife neither wants to have children nor is interested in adopting. He has been dealing with his disappointment with excessive drinking which in turn has affected his work. He insists in talking about Helen's never being home and seems to think that all his problems would be solved if she gave up her evening course and her bridge club.

Comments   Even after much of the emotional load has been dissipated and the client has identified the basic problem there is often a lot of vagueness around the problem. The reasons for the vagueness may be one or more of those listed in the previous chapter on identification.

One of the major challenges in problem clarification is to get the client to take ownership of the problem; to confirm that s/he is part of the problem no matter how many terrible things others may be doing.

Some individuals during stressful times, others as a way of life, tend to become emotionally involved in problems which literally belong to someone else. Often the individual worries about the problem as though it were her own. A more common trait is that of not being able to be objective about who owns what part of the problem. Lots of problems involve co-workers, family members or lovers. It helps, for reasons to be outlined in the paragraphs below, if the client can see which problem and what part of the problem is his own, which belongs to another person in the family or work situation and which are jointly owned by any two or more persons in the system. e.g. (A family finds itself in serious turmoil because they cannot decide on when to take a family camping trip. Both parents work and their regular vacation times don't match. Getting a change of vacation times are problems owned individually by Mom and Dad. The individuals *are powerless* in terms of solving the other person's problem. Each will have to negotiate with their own employer. Any happy solution will be difficult unless Mom and Dad accept their individual responsibility for that part of the family problem.)

Problems are easier to understand and offer some hope of solution when the client boils the problem down into a number of specific parts.

- This procedure provides opportunity for the client to take a first small and winnable step toward a solution. Successful action leads to both hope and improved self-esteem.
- The process of boiling the problem down helps further in that the clarity often permits working on more than one problem, or part of the problem at the same time.

Step by Step
Procedure

1. Encourage the client to tell his story; be curious and when it sounds vague, voice your difficulty in understanding.

2. Ask the client to retell those parts which are vague and request that s/he tell it from a different perspective.

3. Do some reality-testing with the client. Ask for specifics about times and places.

4. Offer to work together at clarifying the various parts of the problem. State one part you see clearly and ask for other parts which s/he can identify. Continue to take turns identifying parts. Don't carry this too far, only long enough to tease out the major parts.

5. Encourage the client to identify ownership. Divide the ownership list into three sections. Those parts which are owned by others, those which he owns (push for ownership where there is obvious denial or avoidance) and those which are owned jointly.

6. Assist the client in understanding that he has considerable power over those parts of the problem he owns and little power to resolve other's problems which may be connected to his problem.

7. Encourage the client by building some realistic hope. Point out that by boiling the problem down he is getting into a position to select priorities and to tackle some winnable part of the total problem.

Bridging

This material can be helpful to first aiders in working on their own personal problems.

It can be used with individuals or groups to help increase productivity and/or job satisfaction.

It can be used by parents, teachers and supervisors.

Warning

Be careful not to do the client's work. Wait for the client's readiness to do the steps.

HELPING CLIENTS TO ESTABLISH PRIORITIES

This section can be used to learn methods of helping a client to understand the importance of working on appropriate and winnable solutions to their problem(s).

Focus

a. Helping the client to develop realistic hope.
b. Helping the clients let go of barriers to solutions, barriers which are beyond their power to change.
c. Preparing the client for eventual selection of some part of the problem to work on where success is fairly certain.
d. Supporting the client when old or new emotions emerge threatening the client's ability to take action steps.

Illustration

Bertha has been irritable and angry for the past four months. There have been some minor behavioral problems with a teenage daughter at home. However, the irritability began about a month after a new department head came to Bertha's place of work. This man reminds her of her dad with whom Bertha fought most of the time when she was in her teens. Bertha has been going out of her way to prove the department head wrong. She gets caught occasionally in a power struggle with her ex-husband over their daughter.

Comments

The patterns people develop in their efforts at solving their problems are sometimes ineffective or downright destructive. These patterns may have been learned first in childhood and are over-laden with old emotions which are often deep-seated and difficult to dislodge. e.g. Bertha in the illustration above. People cannot safely give up old patterns without better self-understanding and then discovering some new pattern to replace the old one.

Discouragement is often a big part of the problem when people go for help. Boiling the problem down into parts, discovering that some of their old efforts at solutions may be wasted energy, and being told that more effective patterns may be available to them becomes a source of hope.

When clients clarify the different parts of the problem, they can be helped to reclaim their feelings of power. They are then able to work on those parts of the problem which are theirs, which they are able to control. In other words, they can select those parts of the problem which promise some real hope for success.

Sometimes during the process of boiling the problem down the client finds himself temporarily flooded with emotions again. This may develop simply as a result of telling the story again. Acceptance of these feelings, together with some realistic encouragement and gentle confrontation, will usually help the client to get through this emotional flooding.

The perspective which the helper brings into the counselling situation through assisting the client to check out the reality of his own situation is reassuring for most emotionally troubled people. It is at this point in the helping relationship that the client needs to establish priorities of the various parts of his problem on the basis of those which he wishes most to resolve. A session on challenging the client to take first steps toward a solution is found on pages 126-127.

Step by Step Procedure

1. Report back to the client by summarizing the different parts of the problem which s/he has clarified for you.
2. Check with the client asking if there is any significant part of the problem which has been overlooked.
3. Ask the client to list for you different things s/he has done in the past in attempts to solve the problem(s). Listen for the patterns which worked as well as for those which did not work.
4. Gently confront the client pointing out the ineffective pattern while offering your own opinion that there may be more effective ways you can discover together.
5. If the client has been working on parts of the problem that are beyond his control, encourage him to focus on areas where he has more control over the outcome of his efforts.
6. Avoid determining your own thoughts about the best solution to the problem.
7. Have the client make a list of the various parts of the problem and then put priorities to each part, giving the highest priorities to those parts which promise successful solution.
8. Turn to pages 128 for more on challenging the client to take action.

Bridging

These materials may be useful for parents, teachers and supervisors.

They apply to group and other organizational situations.

Warning

Avoid imposing *your* priorities on the client and mapping out a set of steps for him/her to follow.

Even if you "know" the best solution, do not weaken the client by doing his/her work.

CONFRONTING A CLIENT TO FOCUS ON THE PROBLEM

Focus
a. Serve as an introduction to the place of confrontation in helping people to help themselves.
b. Help you to learn how to apply the skill of confrontation in assisting with problem clarification.

Illustration
Elmer's excessive drinking has been his way of avoiding the unhappiness in his marriage. Both his wife and his foreman have been complaining about his drinking. He has come to you because he is in real danger of losing his job. A major factor in helping Elmer will be a successful confrontation about his excessive drinking.

Comments
As you proceed through these chapters, you will realize that empathy and emotional support often are of little help by themselves. It is one thing for a parent to kiss the bump on the child's forehead to "make it better", however, it is an entirely different matter to spend hours with a client who continues to complain about other people, or avoids his problem through drinking or some other form of acting out.

There is another type of client for whom all the support in the world will make little difference, the person who gets secondary gain from having his/her problem; i.e. she does not want to give up the problem although she may be going through the motions of getting help. A good example is the chronically depressed person who has learned to get his strokes by having problems. He can manipulate others to feel sorry for him, to let him cling and be dependent on them.

Confrontation becomes a necessary and delicate skill in all of the above situations. In developing a relationship, confrontation which comes too early will drive the client away. The client will either stop getting help altogether or will go to someone else who "understands him better."

On the other hand, if the helper is too soft, the client will soon put most of his energy into manipulation and/or avoidance. As soon as there is some basic trust in the helping relationship and the client has simmered down, it is time to begin gentle confrontation.

Confrontation usually does not begin until the problem clarification stage of helping. One exception is the alcoholic who needs to be told in the first session that you or any other counsellor cannot help him with emotional problems if he comes to the session having been drinking the past twenty-four hours or feeling guilty about having been drinking since the last meeting.

The basic functions of confrontation are

- to get the client to face up to reality.
- to point out the ineffective, or even destructive patterns the client is using to solve his/her problem.

Step by Step Procedure

1. Take time to make certain that the issue or problem you are about to point out to the client is clear to you. (If you are not certain check it out with a peer or consultant before confronting the client.)

2. Check your own interest or motives for using confrontation. Are you angry at the client? Are you trying to point out his "stupidity"? Maybe you just want to show the client how tough you are or to teach him a lesson.

3. Be gentle and supportive, yet firm when you confront. Try something like: "I've noticed that you use a lot of energy blaming your wife for your problem and seldom focus on your part in it. You would have a lot more success if you were to focus on yourself." Or you might try: "I've noticed tears several times as you talk about the disappointment in your marriage, and then you start talking about something else. There must be a lot of feeling behind these tears. Maybe we're getting close to something important."

4. Be clear about what you can and cannot do in helping the client by way of focusing on the problem. Be firm where the avoidance involves patterns which are destructive, like drinking. Present your position clearly and in a way that invites co-operation and offers support. Do not threaten or punish.

5. Since the client usually needs his defensive patterns, to keep his/her sanity, do not strip away his/her defenses. S/he will need his old pattern if he cannot replace it or else he will not be able to cope at all. Gently confront the client to do the work outlined in the two previous sections.

6. Check out *yourself* to see whether you are ready to be a supportive ally as the client faces the pain and reality of his actions.

7. Take your time. There is a danger at this stage of helping, of doing too much of the client's work.

Bridging　　This material on confrontation may be particularly useful in helping alcoholics, certain depressed and/or dependent persons, and with people who manipulate others into taking care of them and/or feeling sorry for them.

　　It can be used also in more normal situations where parenting, teaching or supervision are involved.

Warning　　Do not confuse confronting a client to own and face his problem with the kind of confrontation necessary in challenging a client to take action steps. It is premature to confront for action on a problem that is neither owned by, nor clear to the client.

Supporting while confronting

CHAPTER IV

PART THREE

CHALLENGING THE CLIENT TO COPE

INTRODUCTION

Challenging the client to cope is not effective until the problem or issue has been clarified by the client and the parts of the problem have been listed in order of priority for work. This is the reason for putting this part last in the chapter on "Helping People with Emotional Problems."

Common traps in the helping process include the suggestion of possible solutions prematurely, or encouraging the client to select a goal prematurely before the emotional turmoil has settled down or before the problem is clear.

Section 2 is on skills for timing your challenge to the client to take action steps. Section 3 focuses on helping the client to discover, assess and build up her own inner resources. Section 4 focuses on helping the client to build up external resources through a support system of family, friends, etc.

Section 5 in this part focuses on motivating the resistant client. Section 6 deals with the importance of evaluation as a way of helping the client.

In summary, this part has to do with skills which come under the heading of 'challenging people to cope'. There is more to helping than listening and supporting. It is possible for both the helper and the client to get stuck in an empathic relationship of listening. Assisting the client in defining the problem(s) and challenging the client to begin a workable course of action, to make possible changes becomes an important part of the helping relationship.

Timing interventions which challenge the client to take action steps requires some understanding of the problem solving and decision making process. You do not need a text book or university degree to understand the process. You have been through it many times yourself.

Timing interventions which challenge the client to cope are important in aiding the client's growth and progress. Clients in emotional difficulties are usually open to growth and change once the emotional turmoil settles. One has only to observe small children in how they try, risk and learn new activities, such as walking, to get some sense of the importance of timing. Adults, including helpers, will often short circuit the process through poor timing.

Plenty of helpers who have learned to listen well, often wish that there were something more they could do to get unstuck with the client.

There are helpers who get caught in a very different trap. They need to see action or they are uncomfortable with the client's emotional pain. These helpers often intervene prematurely with a prescribed course of action or quickly promote some step proposed by the client, when the client is not yet clear as to what is the problem.

The ideal client would go through a process which would look like this.

1) He would quickly get into trusting the helper. Talking to the helper, getting support would result in a lot of emotional stability.
2) He would go over his problem, a couple of times with you and would soon be clear on what the problem is.
3) He would see which parts of the problem are his and which belong to others.
4) Now he would be able to tell you clearly what the problem is, how he intends to back off those parts which belong to others.
5) He would set a goal for himself, i.e. the solution he desires.
6) He would set priorities for the steps he plans to take.
7) He would then begin working on the first winnable step.

Part of knowing when to help the client is being able to make an accurate assessment about the client's emotional stability and about his/her problem solving skills.

Every bit as important is the information you get back from the client as you observe him taking on responsibility for helping himself.

TIMING INTERVENTIONS IN CHALLENGING THE CLIENT TO COPE

Focus

a. Develop skills in knowing *when* to help the client in setting goals and taking steps towards achieving those goals.
b. Develop skills in testing the client's ability to take action steps now.
c. Identify how to help the clients to set their own time schedule for achieving their goals.

Illustrations

A. You are feeling stuck with Jean, a forty-five year old woman who came to you two months ago "feeling very down." Jean looks better and is much brighter. However, she does nothing but complain to you about the same old problem of not having any social life. You are getting tired of her complaining and are wondering how to get her moving.

B. Jack is a very anxious workaholic who has been making some mistakes at work. What really got to him a few weeks ago is that his in-laws want him and Joyce to buy their house. Joyce has long wanted to live in a home with a yard and a garden rather than a rented apartment. Joyce's parents are wanting to live in the in-law suite. Jack has been unable to make decisions lately. He cannot negotiate with his wife because of his high level of anxiety about the whole problem. Her parents are saying that they will wait another month for a decision.

Comments

In illustration A, the timing problem arises because the client, who has overcome her depressed feelings, is still going in circles. The first aider does not know what to do next.

In illustration B, there are external pressures of a deadline while the client is still in considerable emotional turmoil. The deadline may serve to increase the emotional storm. Does the first aider wait until the client settles down or does s/he begin to challenge the client to take action steps toward resolution of the problem.

Step by Step Procedure

1. Learn and practice the problem solving procedures listed above in the portrait of the ideal client by applying them to your own problems.

2. Test the client's ability to take some achievable action steps. Check to see if the client is aware of simple things such as time of day, day of week, etc. Note how good the client's memory is, how well s/he keeps appointments, etc. Note whether you feel easier inside when you are with the client. Does it feel more like a normal meeting now? These are but a few of the practical ways to test whether or not the client is ready to be nudged into action.

3. If the client is very helpless you may have to do one of his steps for him. However, in doing this you will likely increase his dependence on you and you will get in the way of him helping himself. Doing it for him will also deprive the client of good feelings about himself.

4. Go over a time schedule with the client. Establish a framework for this schedule by writing in fixed times set by someone else, such as the family coming for Christmas, etc. If your client is pregnant, the baby will not wait twelve months to be born. Encourage your client to set his own time goals.

5. Let the client know that you expect reports of progress to you at appropriate time points. Even if he takes no action, he is to report.

6. Communicate to the client that together you will want to evaluate the whole experience as s/he proceeds with the resolution of the problem.

7. Some helpers trained in listening skills sometimes get stuck because they do not know what to do as a next step. If your client week after week, keeps complaining or just sharing feelings, both of you may be stuck. It is time for the helper to get some supervision and to do some self evaluation.

Bridging

The comments and procedures in this section apply to teaching situations where goals are involved. e.g. Planning for retirement, for a change of career, for a vacation or for a change of life style.

Warning

- The most common trap the helper gets into around timing is one of prematurely pushing the client to work on what the helper thinks would be a good solution.
- You should not expect from the client more than s/he is capable of doing and coping.

HELPING THE CLIENT DEVELOP INNER RESOURCES

Focus

a. Learn how to assist your client in doing an inventory of his/her resources.
b. Learn how to encourage your client to develop new inner resources necessary for coping with life.

Illustration

Jim has worked with the company for 15 years. He is a machinist and recently was promoted to foreman. He has lots of skills, but has always been shy and apologetic about himself. Since his promotion, he has become depressed and if he doesn't improve, he will be demoted to his old position. His superior believes in him and has suggested that he call you for help. You have had three meetings with him and talking has helped lessen his depressed feelings. You sense that this is not enough for Jim, that there is something more he and you can do about the problem. Jim needs you to help him rediscover his own inner resources, so he can make better use of them.

Comments

People who have been criticized a lot as children or youth, who have had a series of failures, usually have difficulty in believing in themselves and often feel inadequate.

Such feeling of inadequacy can lead to two extreme behavior patterns. One is to take no risk or initiatives in solving the problems. The other extreme is to react to their feelings of inadequacy by taking on tasks that are beyond their ability in an effort to prove themselves.

Crucial to breaking one's negative pattern is making an accurate inventory of inner resources and weaknesses. Rather than have someone else do the inventory for us, it is far more acceptable if we do it for ourselves.

People under extreme stress as well as those who have very low opinions of themselves often are unable to believe that they have strength and inner resources. Part of the task in helping these people do an inventory is encouraging them to own and claim their strengths.

Any accurate inventory of inner strength will also include the identification of weaknesses and shortcomings. In selecting which resources we wish to develop, it is important that we keep in mind the principle of choosing achievable realistic goals.

Step by Step Procedure

1. Once you have achieved a relationship with the client, as you work together on problem clarification, focus on how much the client is failing to use available inner resources and to what extent needed resources are missing.

2. When you realize that the client has resources s/he is not using, confront the client with your observation, using only one obvious instance as an example. Do *not* offer a list of your observations.

3. Invite the client to join you in a bragging exercise. Ask him to tell you up to ten strengths he has, good things that might be useful in relation to his problem.

4. Once the client has come up with several strengths, tell him the strengths you have heard from him. If you have some of those qualities, tell the client but keep *your* list short.

5. Encourage the client to think of others which he may have missed. Then feed back what you hear.

6. Ask the client to write down the resources s/he has identified.

7. Have the client tell you which resources he has been using and when he last used particular resources.

8. Together identify useful resources which would be helpful but are not on the list.

9. Explore with the client practical and realistic goals for acquiring a particular resource, e.g. a sense of humor, or skills in decision making, or ability to confront.

Bridging   The comments and procedures in this section have been tried and found useful in the following situations:
- Small groups of persons who are wanting to improve their confidence and self-image.
- Persons who tend to under-utilize their skills and resources.
- Pairs of peers or friends who want to help each other to greater awareness of their inner resources.

Warning   Clients who are dependent on others or those who do a lot of blaming have difficulty with these steps. They tend to believe that others will solve their problems or that others are responsible for their problems and they do not really need to look at themselves. Sometimes it's a real fear that they will find nothing but shortcomings. These people will need your support, or perhaps even professional help to deal with their blocks.

HELPING CLIENTS BUILD UP EXTERNAL RESOURCES

Focus

a. Illustrate the importance of external support systems.
b. Learn how to assist your clients in doing an inventory.
c. Help the client to take steps in building up a support system.

Illustration

Mary works full time, has three teenagers, and her husband recently walked out on them. Her nearest relatives live three thousand miles away. Her marriage has been in poor shape for three years since they moved to town so they made no couple friends. Her job, housework and kids gave her reason to refrain from making her own friends.

Mary is literally in a panic now and hardly able to do her job. When she comes to you for help, all you know is that her husband has left and she has three teenagers. As she talked about her anxiety and pain, you picked up that you are about the only "friend" she has to talk to; you are the only person giving her emotional support.

Comments

There is lots of proven evidence available today to indicate that loneliness, inadequate numbers of friends, relatives and neighbors are major causes of both physical and emotional illness.

A major task of every helper is to encourage and instruct the lonely and loners of our society in building support around them. Research evidence has confirmed that loneliness, isolation and the lack of friends contribute to emotional illness.

Research done in the Boston area more than twenty-five years ago showed that the people in crisis who had more other people in their support system came through the crisis sooner and survived it better than those people who had fewer other people.

Likewise, another study done on the West Coast showed that the average healthy person has about twenty-five others while the mentally ill person has only seven others.

Step by Step Procedure

1. Prepare an inventory of your own support system, in order to understand the importance of a support system for your client. How many persons would be available to you for support or companionship during a crisis? Is your system adequate?

2. Assuming you know your client a bit, you are ready to help him look at his support system. Tell your client your observations, not opinions, of his support system.

3. Ask the client to make a list of the people who are in his/her support system. Request that s/he make some notes of the availability of each person.

4. If the client is not using available persons, not reaching out and asking for support, point this out. Be firm, confronting and supportive, but do not accept excuses.

5. Encourage the client to select a few persons and to begin asking for support and companionship.

6. Have the client, a) make a list of places to go to meet people and b) to note how s/he might begin building up a support system. Do not offer your suggestions until you have evidence that the client is actually working and producing his own list and notes.

7. Encourage the client to take some first achievable steps on his own and to report back to you.

8. It is important to contract with the client to set a date to report back to you on any actions s/he has agreed to take toward any of the above steps.

9. As the client develops more external resources, he will need you less, for he will look after emotional needs in the normal ways utilized by average people day by day.

Bridging

The material in this chapter can be used with people who have recently moved to a new community. It can be used with people whose children are about to leave the nest. Or it can be used in preparation for retirement.

Warning

A few individuals have had little or no experience in social situations. Their skills are few and far between. Some others are really afraid of closeness. Do not give up on these slow starters, simply use good sense in nudging them into action, remembering that their own pace may be somewhat different than yours.

MOTIVATING THE RESISTANT CLIENT

Focus

a. Learn ways to use resistance rather than getting stuck or in giving up.
b. Discover the importance of using the client's resistance as a way of helping him to help himself.
c. Learn ways to identify your own response to the client's resistance.

Illustration

Irma is forty-five years old, single, lives alone and has worked for her company as a secretary for twenty years. She has always tended to get attention by complaining about a lot of little things. Her complaining increased about six months ago after her mother died. The other people in her department decided to 'gang up' on her, being tired of her complaining. Irma came to you and after six or seven meetings had stopped a lot of the complaining. She began to see that she needed attention and affection. You were expecting that she would start doing something by way of making friends and getting out.

However, Irma has become anxious about moving to a new apartment and has started complaining again. She is now complaining to you that the counselling isn't helping her any. Unless you talk about the resistance, she could simply leave and not return, thus missing an opportunity to improve her life.

Comments

Resistance is used by the client as a way of blocking progress or change. Frequently the client is unaware of blocking or, if aware, has some rational explanation about what is happening.

The blocking can take the form of stubborn silence, changing the topic, forgetting appointments, getting into some new kind of trouble, reverting back to old patterns (which had disappeared).

Generally, resistance is a means used by the client to regain some measure of comfort or control, in the face of fear; the fear of getting too close to "hot" feelings or the fear of change. As ineffective, destructive, maybe even painful, as old coping patterns may be for the client, there is some comfort in maintaining them; it is all he knows!

Responding to the client with one's own anger and frustration only makes matters worse and both get stuck in the confrontation. What will work though is an approach which has two clearly related steps.

The *first* step is to become aware of and respond to the fear behind the resistance. For help in doing this refer back to the chapter on listening and pick up on your skills in listening to and responding to feelings. e.g. You can respond to the non-verbal clues provided by the client who has stopped talking and gives you only silence.

The *second* step is to talk about the fear behind the resistance. Once the client knows that you understand and care s/he may be able to look at and talk about the feelings. Then later you will be able to point out to the client how the client was using resistance behaviour in an honest effort to protect against the feared pain and discomfort.

Part Three   **Challenging the Client to Cope**

Step by Step Procedure

1. When faced with resistance reflect on your own feelings.
2. Review what you know about the client as a total person to get some picture of what fear and other feelings may be behind the resistance.
3. If you sense that the client is of a very antisocial type, check out your hunch with a professional. Antisocial personalities are usually very clever and cunning. There is no way that you will be able to work with the resistance. These people have little interest in responding to or in improving through counselling or therapy.
4. Begin listening and responding to the feelings and fear behind the resistance.
5. After the feelings are acceptable to the client and the fear has eased, begin to explore together. Point out to the client what you observed in the resistant behaviour without passing judgment. Invite the client to explore with you what it is all about.
6. Together you can now move back to wherever you were with the problem identification or problem resolution. *You will have both learned from the interruption.*
7. Evaluate your own responses to the resistance. Explore whether or not you took the resistance personally, and how you were different as a helper when you understood the resistance as part of the client's struggle.
8. Take some time to reflect on resistance in the client as an opportunity for working together toward health and resolution of the problem.

Bridging

What you discover in this session may also apply to certain sytems, like families, groups or departments. This section does not apply to the unwilling client who has been sent and simply does not want to be there. It applies to those situations where the client has expressed interest in changing for the better. The group or client may want change but is afraid of change and does not want to give up "the way I/we used to do it."

Warning

Beware of 'beating your head against a brick wall' with those clients whose life style is close to total manipulation of others. Antisocial personalities are of this type. Alcoholics who are not doing anything about their sobriety either through AA or elsewhere, will not work with you on their resistance.

LEARNING HOW TO EVALUATE

Focus
  a. Learn that in assisting the client to evaluate you are contributing to his/her future mental health. (In this sense evaluation is not a first aid skill.)
  b. Learn effective evaluation skills.

Illustration
    Hazel and you have had five meetings together. She is a single parent with three boys. The boys are ages eleven to fifteen. She came to you in a panic two days after her fifteen year old got caught at school dividing up some dope with four of his friends. She was unable to go to work the first day because she was beside herself. Once she cooled down she made a number of creative changes in relation to her children and her ex-husband who lives in a nearby town. There are problems still with her son at school, and it will be seven years before the youngest son is through school. In the previous meeting Hazel got angry at you because she thought that you were criticizing her parenting.

Comments
    Evaluation in the helping process has three important functions.
- It aids one to learn from the experience.
- Evaluation can be a help in getting unstuck when there is some issue in the helping relationship as in the above example.
- Evaluation has the effect of providing some sense of direction. "If you are going to know where you are going you have to know where you have been."

We would differentiate between this kind of evaluation and the problem clarification described in Part Two pp. 00. What is of interest is the experience the client is having as s/he shares with you and works on the resolution of the problem. The client may be helped to evaluate the steps s/he is taking toward resolution of the problem. Together you may evaluate the experience you have had and are still having in the helping relationship.

    A most important goal in all helping, except in ongoing supportive relationships with some of the emotionally handicapped people, is to arrive at the time when the client no longer needs you. In the next section, I will touch on evaluation as part of the process of ending a helping relationship.

Evaluate to know where you are going

Step by Step
Procedure 1. Early in establishing the helping relationship let the client know that you expect to do some evaluation together along the way.

2. Introduce the first experience of evaluation at the close of the first meeting with something like "let's talk for a minute or two about how this meeting has been for you." If it seems important, end every meeting in a similar manner.

3. Whenever the client reports either exciting success with something s/he has done about the problem, take time before the end of the session to get the client to talk about his/her contribution to the success. Do the same with disappointments and perceived failures. Be careful not to be judgmental.

4. Whenever you feel that you and the client have been on a flat plateau, going nowhere, introduce evaluation as a way of getting things going again. This may lead to a referral or to termination.

5. Introduce and use evaluation as a way of testing whether it is appropriate to begin ending the helping relationship.

6. If one of your helping goals is to aid the client in gaining improved mental health and ability to cope with life without you then you must introduce evaluation as a major part of the termination (ending session) you have together.

Bridging The material in this session overlaps with the section on referrals and endings (pp. 139). It can be used in working with groups or with committees, or in a great variety of team-work situations.

Warning If you do the evaluation work of the client, then you may not only deprive the client of an opportunity to grow, but you may damage the helping relationship.

SUCCESSFULLY ENDING A HELPING RELATIONSHIP

Focus

a. When termination is appropriate.
b. The importance of dealing with endings.
c. Appropriate "good-byes".

Illustration

You are meeting with Elsie for the third time. You were expecting that she might bring up the question of termination. As she was leaving the previous session, she mentioned having seen you and her supervisor together at lunch.

At the beginning of this session she announces that she doesn't need your help anymore. Yet Elsie had very serious problems two weeks ago. Is this termination appropriate? How do you find out?

An unsuccessful ending

Comments   People tend to end helping relationships using the same patterns they use when they end other relationships.

Some people tend to end relationships prematurely.

Others hang on too long.

Some leave without saying good-bye.

Some actually leave but hang on to the relationship emotionally (often with destructive results).

An ordinary, yet meaningful ending, is experienced by the graduate from high school or the lad who is playing his very last ball game with the team.

The death of a close friend or of a family member is more traumatic. So is the loss of one's ability to play sports through a permanent back injury.

All the little and medium endings in life serve as important preparation for the more traumatic endings. The experience in the little endings help to set the pattern for how one copes with the unexpected and often tragic endings.

The termination experience the client has with the helper is an opportunity for lasting growth and new ability to cope with "endings" further down the road in the client's life. Many people who experience emotional difficulties have had unhappy endings in the past and may have developed a pattern of avoiding the feelings that go with endings or may even avoid the ending itself and just not come any more; no reasons given. There are helpers who out of their tendency to avoid endings, aid and abet the client in the avoidance. It becomes important therefore, for the helper to understand his/her own patterns around endings. Read the section on losses and endings, in Chapter V (pp. 149).

Knowing when termination is appropriate is a skill which comes from experience. Premature termination may be initiated by the client for one of the following reasons.

- The client knows the helper will later introduce the fact of termination and will leave first as a way of avoiding the hurt.
- Some type of tension, discomfort or misunderstanding has emerged in the helping relationship.
- The counselling got too close to some fearful feeling or issue.

Evaluation is part of any creative termination. The helper may remind the client of the goals you agreed to work on. However the client needs to do most of the evaluation. With your encouragement the client can tell you:

- how well the goals were reached.
- what disappointments were experienced.
- what the overall experience was like.
- what tasks remain for the client to work on out there.
- what s/he expects it will be like without the regular meetings.

The helper can bring fairness and reality to the ending by sharing his/her own satisfactions, disappointments and feelings about the ending. However, helpers need to be careful not to do the client's work at this point.

Appropriate final good-byes involve being clear that this is the last meeting and acknowledging any "dragging of the feet" in saying good-bye. A handshake, an embrace whichever seems appropriate and then walking away, closing the door or some clear symbol that this is the end.

Step by Step Procedure

1. Listen for verbal clues and watch for non-verbal clues which may indicate a premature termination.

2. If the helping relationship is being prolonged beyond what is necessary, talk to yourself or better still, to a peer or supervisor.

3. With either step 1 or 2 completed, it's now time to talk to your client about what is happening in the helping relationship. In any case, attempt to get to the feelings or concerns behind the behaviour.

4. If it's been getting "too hot" for the client, reassure him/her that it will be okay and that it will be better to remain and to move ahead at a comfortable pace rather than to stop with things unresolved.

5. If the imminent termination is because of a problem between you, assure the client that you really care to know what it is and that you can team together to resolve the matter.

6. When both the client and helper agree that termination is appropriate, then it's time to set up a procedure for evaluating and saying good-bye.

7. You now do the evaluation together.
    a) Begin with the original goals.
    b) Have the client list goals reached, together with disappointments.
8. Encourage the client to continue helping him/ herself with any unfinished business.
9. You then say good-bye in whatever way is appropriate, making sure it is clear and final.
10. In situations where there is a referral, you may contract to continue with support until the referral is completed.
11. In situations where you work or where social activities will bring you together, it is important to end the 'helping' relationship as such. This should leave you both clear about the difference between the two kinds of relationships.

Bridging   The principles and skills outlined here would apply to ending those relationships where there have been some type of contract, covenant or agreement. The focus in all situations would be on evaluating goals worked on, surfacing feelings related to endings and acceptance of the end of the relationship.

Warning   Clients who have difficulty with endings are quick to sense whether the helper has difficulty, too. Learning skills in how to help the client get the most out of endings will be of no help without some real self-insight by the helper in the area of how s/he handles endings, losses and terminations.

CHAPTER V

SPECIAL SITUATIONS

INTRODUCTION

This chapter of the manual covers special situations. Developing skills in these situations will make things a lot easier for you when faced with them.

One section focuses on the most important skill of them all; the skill of being able to keep confidential everything your client shares with you.

Materials having to do with the following situations are provided in this chapter:
- a short list of resources
- support for the emotionally handicapped
- post emergency follow up
- working with the alcoholic
- client's responses to losses
- the helper gets help and
- confidentiality.

Which one is the mental health professional?

SHORT LIST OF RESOURCES

The availability of resources depends on a number of factors:

Rural or *large city*

Remoteness from the centres

Affluence of the community. Often the middle class has the least resources for emotional emergencies.

How to go about finding the resource you need for making referrals depends in part on where you live and in part on where to turn to ask for information about available resources. Simply because a professional doesn't know about a particular resource does not mean that it's not there.

The lists below focus on where to turn for information about what's available.

Where to Go in Rural Areas

Minister or priest Medical Doctor
School Counsellor Hospital Chaplain
Welfare Office Hospital Social Worker
Human Resources Office Any self-help group
Ex-social worker Ex-psychologist

Most practicing mental health professionals prefer to live in the suburbs. However, do not overlook a very important development of recent years. More and more professionals from this field have moved to the country to get away from it all. These people are a gold mine for emotional first aiders!

Where to Go in the Small Town

A crisis line	Medical doctor
Minister or priest	School Counsellor
Psychiatrist	Psychologist

The welfare or human resources office

The hospital [look for chaplain or social worker]

Nurses who go to homes [check yellow pages]

Local Mental Health Association

The older small town usually has a network of information services which works quite well.

The newer growing towns are often without adequate resources. Furthermore, those people who are providing services often do not know who else is providing services.

Where to Go in the Large Cities and Suburbs

The most obvious sources of information are twofold:

1) *Information Services* listed in the yellow pages of the telephone directory under *Information Bureau*.

2) *Directory of Services* published and updated by a community agency. One of the information services will be able to tell you where to get a copy and how much it costs.

Your local library should have a copy. These directories usually have a subject index as well as a clearly organized table of contents.

POST EMERGENCY FOLLOW UP

Focus
a. A checklist for you to use in making certain that you provide adequate follow up.
b. Help in determining when follow up is important.

Illustration

You were the first aider who responded to the call for help from Etta's husband. Etta was falling apart as she waited for surgery on a lump under her arm. You not only listened to her concerns, but you supported her in going to see her family doctor that same day to get information about some of her unanswered questions. The emergency ended after her talk with the doctor.

Comments

In the illustration above, several questions should be considered by the first aider now that the emergency is over.

- Will Etta find herself in another emergency before the operation?
- If no emergency develops, could Etta benefit through a few more opportunities to talk with you before the operation?
- In view of her reluctance to talk over private matters and to ask for support, how do you approach her so that she does not turn down your offer?
- How will things be for Etta after the surgery and after she comes home from the hospital?
- What about an evaluation together of the whole helping experience which you both shared? Might this be a way of Etta learning to be more open with people in her support system when she has concerns?

Those people who have come through a crisis in life and are more able than ever before to handle future crises will have:

- had an adequate support system, both in numbers and competency.
- had support when they needed it.
- evaluated the experience and learned from it.

Having support when they need it includes having support during the post emergency period. If a first aider provides that support, then s/he should know:

- when *not* to terminate the relationship.
- when to intervene once the professional has terminated.

- when to get out of the picture and not be in the way of the client helping himself.
- how to help the client evaluate the experience and thus to contribute to valuable learning of new skills for both the client and yourself.

Step by Step Procedure

1. Determine whether the emergency is over. Use the section on knowing when it's an emergency for your guidelines. pp. 00.

2. If it's over, check out the following and select those steps which are important for this particular situation.
   - Are professionals available as needed?
   - Does the client need on-going, non-professional support so as to prevent another emergency happening soon?
   - Is there likely to be a critical time in the days or weeks ahead as things work out? When will it be critical?
   - Who will be available for either on-going support and/or for the critical time(s)?
   - Has the client evaluated the experience so that s/he can be stronger next time?
   - When would be the best time to evaluate?
   - Am I willing to be involved as necessary and appropriate?

3. Do those things that are necessary providing you are willing, available and capable.

4. Be firm and tactful when the client resists help. See pp. 133.

5. Support the client in getting some other helper if you cannot do those important tasks.

6. Do terminate in a helpful way. See pp. 141 on Successfully Ending a Helping Relationship.

Bridging

The following sections will be useful in doing post emergency follow up.

All of Part One, Chapter IV.

All of Part Three, Chapter IV with emphasis on Sections 6 and 7.

Warning

During post emergency follow up, you must be clear about your role as distinct from the responsibilities of any professionals involved.

You have an opportunity to support the prescriptions given by the professionals. Do not scuttle that opportunity!

CLIENT'S RESPONSES TO ENDINGS AND LOSSES

Focus

a. Underscore the importance of helping clients to face losses and work through grief.
b. Learn how to get to feelings generated by endings in both helper and client.
c. Motivate the client to take responsibility for letting go.

Illustrations

A. You have been providing supportive counselling for Merle who has been living in the same place for 20 years. She was severely upset five years ago for a period after the death of her only child. You get together once a month, mostly to talk about her ability to cope on the job and how she feels about herself. She is doing well and really doesn't need the support any longer. Others need your time more.

B. Art was in a severe accident four years ago. He had some brain damage but does well at his job as a bookkeeper, except that he gets confused when under much stress. You are available to him for a chat when he needs you. He became very upset when he discovered that you will be leaving the company and moving to another province in four months.

Comments   In illustration A, Merle, like a lot of emotionally troubled people, found herself unable to cope with some rather common crises in her life because of earlier big losses in her life. Her mother died when she was four, that was the first big loss. She used to get depressed every time she moved. Years later her only child was killed in an accident.

Many people whom we help have difficulty with losses and endings. When the helping relationship ends they can
- continue to grow in strength, or
- be no stronger or able to cope than when they started (however the current crisis is over), or
- be much less able to handle future crises.

It is fairly common in helping situations for things to deteriorate after the idea of termination has surfaced, whether it was brought up by the helper or the client. It is also common for everyone involved to avoid the feelings generated by the idea of termination. This avoidance can be the real cause of the deterioration and setback.

Sometimes these clients will create a new problem as a way of avoiding termination. Helpers also have been known to hang on to their clients, reasoning that the client still needs help. Whatever patterns emerge at termination time, it is safe to assume that the client may have slipped back to well-used, but ineffective ways of handling losses.

The skillful helper can help the client to turn things around this time with the termination experience being a valuable new learning. However, that will not happen if both the helper and the client ignore and avoid the feelings generated by the loss.

It is important to create opportunities to evaluate as outlined on pp. 136. The helper needs to be aware of the following:
- Feelings about the ending itself.
- Possible anger at the helper, mixed with affection and gratitude.
- Anxiety about making it on his/her own without the helper.
- Avoidance of the feelings by not saying "good-bye" and attempting to set up some fuzzy contract for the future. Note how often people say "I'll be seeing you" when there is little likelihood of that happening within any reasonable time, if ever.

Confrontation skills outlined in earlier chapters will aid the helper in getting these issues to the surface where the client can learn and experience more creative ways of facing endings and losses.

Step by Step

Procedure

1. Reflect on how you as a person usually handle endings. If you sense that you have blind spots, talk to another helper about how you experience endings.

2. When the issue of termination comes up, remember who initiated the matter and in what circumstances. You will be able to use this information later in the interest of your client's growth.

3. When it's clear that the client has accepted and acknowledged that termination will take place, communicate clearly to the client that you will want to a) talk over what you have done together, b) explore what the client may wish to do after termination by way of further helping him/herself, and c) that you will want to share together how each of you experience and feel about the termination of the relationship you have developed.

4. If your client agrees to the above, then you take responsibility for seeing that there is plenty of opportunity to evaluate, explore and share feelings about this and other losses.

5. If you are actually terminating, follow the steps on pp. 136 regarding evaluating with the client.

6. To learn by talking about losses and endings, get into the feelings. You can do this by responding to feelings expressed verbally or non-verbally, or initiating something like "we all have feelings about losses and endings, perhaps we could share how we feel about the anticipated end of this relationship."

7. Encourage the client to compare these feelings with how s/he managed losses in the past.

8. When it comes to the last meeting, follow the procedures on pages 139 and you will both be richer for having faced and accepted the reality of the loss.

Bridging

The material in this session applies to most situations in life where endings are involved. People who leave or transfer from their place of employment, dismissal of employees, end of a marriage or other relationship, death, closing out a committee, task force or working team, all present situations where loss and feelings around loss are involved.

Warning

The step by step procedures above will not be useful where your relationship with the client has been brief and no real relationship has developed.

SUPPORTIVE COUNSELLING FOR THE EMOTIONALLY HANDICAPPED

Focus

This section can be used to learn about the importance of supportive counselling.

Illustration

Bill developed epileptic attacks when he was twelve. It took about four years of medical research and care before his attacks stopped completely. He is still on medication. He has a job, but he has no social skills and appears to have suffered some permanent emotional damage. A major problem is finding a living situation for him where he will get some emotional support and some guidance. He needs support in order to maintain what self-confidence he has.

Comments

Many of us at some point in life develop a handicap. We had difficulty in seeing clearly at distances. We learned to wear glasses to drive a car, or to watch a movie. We learned to accept our dependency on eye glasses in those situations.

Likewise there are people who are emotionally handicapped and who need on-going support. They do not need first aid so much as they need adequate support systems. It is not so much the advanced training of the supportive helper that counts as it is the quality of the supportive relationship. A creative relationship will make all the difference to how well these persons cope with everyday life in general.

Just as important to their coping is the extent to which they are permitted and encouraged to lead normal lives at work, at home and out in the community. For a lot of these people some of the modern medications have made the difference between institutional care and living in the community. The medication does not create health. The medication tends to relieve the emotional turmoil to the extent that the person in contact with his/her support system creates his own health and ability to cope.

Identifying the Emotional Handicapped

It is not up to you or to me to determine on our own that an individual is emotionally handicapped on a permanent basis. Such an evaluation should be done by people who know what they are doing and should always include a number of such professionals. Chapter III, Section 2, on referrals will help you in getting such assistance. There are individuals who need to be evaluated by a pyschiatrist before you or I make any commitment to helping them. Any report from a certified mental health professional should be taken seriously.

With increased community acceptance, people who have handicaps or who are very dependent on medication tend to report freely about their handicap. If you suspect that an individual is on medication or is in the care of a mental health professional, it is important that you ask direct questions about the medication and who s/he is seeing.

Many individuals who were once hospitalized receive support from groups and or programs provided by the local Mental Health Association. Society, including some corporations, government and community organizations, do believe that people attain a greater measure of health when they live in the community rather than in mental health institutions, and that it is less costly in dollars and cents.

It is suggested that you read the section in Chapter III on what to do when a client needs a psychiatrist or similar medical attention. Remember, at this point, you are learning about supportive counselling for the emotionally handicapped. Supportive counselling has many benefits.

For this to be effective, there are some specific things to learn and to watch for which I will outline in the step by step procedures.

Step by Step
Procedure 1. Check your tolerance for having clients dependent on you. Helpers who take on too many people with on-going dependency needs will burn out quicker than working with people who are able to help themselves.

2. Get some insight into your own patterns in working with dependent people, i.e. Do you tend to give too much and then silently resent what you are doing?

3. Set limits on the number of emotionally handicapped you will see in proportion to your total number of clients.

4. Watch your expectations when working with the emotionally handicapped. You take responsibility away from the client when you do too much and expect too little. On the other hand, you set both yourself and the client up when you expect too much of the client.

5. Know your role concerning the client's medication. You are not a doctor and you have no business trying to be a medical person. However, you have a very important role with the emotionally handicapped who are on medication. Often these people have either forgotten the original directions from their doctor, or they did not understand in the first place, or some of them may have decided to be their own doctors and have either stopped or have increased the dosage. Some have been influenced by well meaning relatives or friends.

   Your role is to encourage the client to stay with the doctor's instructions and prescription. If you have any reason to believe that the client has misunderstood, or is fooling around with or has stopped the medication, tell the client you want him/her to talk to the doctor as soon as possible.

6. If you have any doubts or misgivings about the prescribed medication, do not communicate your doubts to the client. Instead simply tell your client that as a matter of procedure, you are requesting that s/he review the medication with a physician, or with a specialist.

7. Exercise your responsibility to encourage all your clients, particularly those who are emotionally handicapped to maintain a good-sized support system. If they are short, push them to build a larger one. Do *not* accept the client's resistance to doing something about it. Dependent clients have a way of seducing helpers into thinking that they alone 'understand'.

   Keep in mind that most communities have competent and oft-times trained volunteers who can be useful to the emotionally handicapped.

8. Make sure that you get to know some of the other people in his/her support system. Insist on getting the client's permission to consult with a few of these others. Consult with doctors, AA sponsors, etc. Beware of consulting behind the client's back without his/her knowledge of the nature of the consultation.

9. At this point, it would be well to read the section on confidentiality.

Bridging   The step by step procedures above apply to many situations where there is a physical handicap whether or not there is an emotional handicap.

Warning
- Remember, even with people who need to depend on you, the principle of helping people to help themselves is still extremely important.
- Watch for your own negative feelings about particular emotional handicaps. Let someone else provide the support in those situations. Later, you may do something about resolving those negative feelings.

Know and respect your limitations

WORKING WITH THE ALCOHOLIC

Focus

a. Improve your understanding of the defense patterns used by the alcoholic client.
b. Develop skills that will enable you to attain a better batting average when counselling the alcoholic.
c. Improve your skills in utilizing other support for the client. e.g. Alcoholics Anonymous

Illustration

Jim has been a heavy drinker for years. Until recently, it showed only on the job on Mondays, the result of heavy week-end drinking. For the past three months he has been drinking every day. This change came about right after his father died. He smells of alcohol and is a bit unsteady when he comes to talk with you.

Comments

Alcoholism is not only a widespread problem in our society, it is one of the most difficult for both professional and para-professional helpers to work with. Several patterns used by the average alcoholic make things difficult for the helper.

- The alcoholic uses denial as a way of avoiding his problem(s).
- There is usually an internal conflict over the child-like need to be dependent. The alcoholic fights this by being extremely independent (counter-dependent).
- The alcoholic reasons out his/her problems with "alcoholic thinking". This thinking involves all sorts of inappropriate excuses for drinking.
- The alcoholic often acts out strong feelings of guilt.
- Perhaps, most difficult for the helper, is the manipulation used by the alcoholic. They will play on your sympathy or use some other method to "make you part of their problem" rather than change themselves.

There is a widespread belief in our society that alcoholics have to reach "rock-bottom" before they can be helped. Yet there are many opportunities to help the alcoholic to help himself with related or underlying problems before bottom is reached. The catch twenty-two in working with the alcoholic is that it is futile to work on the emotions and the underlying problems unless the client stops drinking. If you get involved in "getting him dry," you will never get to work together on either the emotions or the other problems.

I have worked out a model of working with alcoholics that results in a high success rate. I offer to establish a helping relationship with the alcoholic to work together on the emotions and other problems, *only* if the client makes a *commitment* to get an AA sponsor, get on antabuse as a medication or get into a reliable drug-addiction program. I require a structure where I can check the commitment and, if I find the client is not keeping the commitment, I will terminate the counselling. Basically, this results in the client remaining sober or having to deal with "slips" elsewhere and we are free to focus on our counselling goals.

One difficulty helpers encounter is with the client who is a borderline alcoholic who also denies that there is a drinking problem. The helper needs clear definitions of alcoholism and objective sources of information in order to make a decision about whether or not to apply the above requirements.

You can use the AA definition as one measure. Contact your local AA for their checklist. The medical definition divides alcoholism into three categories:
1) Alcoholic addiction.
2) Episodic excessive drinking.
3) Habitual excessive drinking.

With information from sources other than the client, together with your observations, it is not so difficult to identify the alcoholic client. If there has been excessive habitual drinking for a continuous period of at least three months, simply tell that client that you will not work with him/her unless one of the above requirements is met.

Treat the binge drinking differently. Request that they not come to an appointment if they have been drinking during the previous twenty-four hours.

Apply the more rigid requirement to the habitual excessive drinking client. More time is needed to gather the information in order to distinguish between this category and the binge drinking. A good yardstick is the medical definition, "An alcoholic who is obviously under the influence more than once a week or who is intoxicated more than twelve times yearly."

In gathering the information and in the subsequent contracting, the helper must be firm, gentle and caring with the client, all at the same time.

Step by Step Procedure

1. If you know there is drinking, face the client with that awareness early in the first meeting.

2. Before the first meeting ends, make it clear to the client that you are interested in helping with his/her problems, but that you will not take on the task of helping him/her control any drinking problem.

3. Gather as much information as you can about the client's drinking patterns and the amount of drinking. Tell the client that it is important for you to know this about him/her in order to help with the other problems.

4. Also in the first meeting, ask the client for permission to talk to people about the drinking patterns. If the client refuses, inform him/her that you cannot help without full and accurate information. Do not allow yourself to be manipulated at this point.

5. If you are certain, by the end of the first meeting, that the client is an alcoholic or an excessive habitual drinker request that before the next meeting s/he become involved in one of the three required programs. Further, request that at the next meeting he provide you with the name of the AA sponsor, the prescribing doctor, or the counsellor in the drug addiction program.

6. Make sure that you talk to that other helper before you agree to any on-going counselling with the client. Usually these other helpers are glad to learn about your role with the client. The AA sponsor will be open to meeting together with you and the client to clarify your roles.

7. Stay clear about your role with the client. As you spell out the role and your goals, make it clear again that you do not wish to get involved in whether the client drinks or not, that it is between the client and the other helper. However, be firm about the client maintaining a regular relationship with the other helper.

8. If and when the client drinks, accept it and tell the client to work through his bad feelings with the other helper. Do not accept any termination of the relationship with the other helpers.
9. Work at not getting caught in the client's problems with dependent needs. With this approach, the client is caught in a catch-22 situation. The client has to take steps to end the drinking problem or s/he loses the one helping relationship where the concern is about his emotions and life's problems, and where his drinking does not become an issue.

Bridging   Many of the principles and suggestions in this chapter apply to a person addicted to either illegal or prescription drugs. A number of alcoholics are already on drugs while others change to drug addiction when they stop drinking.

Warning   Be aware of any tendency on your part to think that you can get the alcoholic to stop drinking. Furthermore, watch out for distorted expectations you have of yourself about being able to help the alcoholic client while s/he continues the excessive alcoholic drinking.

THE IMPORTANCE OF CONFIDENTIALITY

Your clients, like your closest friends, put their trust in you and confide personal information and feelings. They deserve complete confidentiality.

Focus
a. Impress on you the importance of keeping confidentiality.
b. Help you become aware of some seemingly innocent traps.

Illustration   You have seen a sixteen year old daughter of an acquaintance. In her need to talk, she really unloaded a lot in the first session. You did not get around to telling her how you would handle confidentiality if her parents called. Mum did call and all you told her was that you and Cathy got on well and that you expected her for another session. Cathy did not return. Although you did not break confidentiality, you had not made that clear to her during the first meeting. She was afraid of your telling her mother her innermost thoughts.

Comments   Persons who need emotional first aid have a need to share their feelings, fears and inner thoughts as well as to confess behavior they would not report to others. In short, they need to be able to *trust* you.

There is the problem of what you actually do with the confidential information. Then there is the problem of what the client fears you may do or have done with it.

In any situation, such as in a corporation, where the client is accountable to others to whom you have access, the situation is fraught with *real* and *imagined* dangers.

There are situations where some other person such as a spouse, parent, lawyer or police may attempt to get information from you. They sometimes go after the information out of their own panic and may attempt to trick you into providing the information.

Helpers need to be clear themselves about their own principles and ability to keep confidentiality. They must inform their clients about their practice around confidentiality. With new clients, it is not enough to assume that they know without your telling them. Check out to see if they have any concerns.

If for some reason you need to talk to another helper about the client such as a family doctor or parent, be sure to get the client's permission; in writing is best.

If you have a peer or consultant to whom you turn for help and/or from whom you receive training, inform your clients that you have this support. Do not ever put yourself into situations where you cannot turn for help. Assure the client that this is normal practice for you and that you will maintain appropriate confidentiality.

When I am in situations where I am contracted to provide any kind of report on the client, I follow certain principles and procedures. I tell the client that I don't like being in the situation and that I assume that we both are equal at that point. Although I do not permit the client to formulate the report, I show the client the report, before I give the report.

This gives me an opportunity to respond to the client's feelings and opinions about the report in a helpful, caring and firm way.

Another principle to follow is this: Do not provide any unnecessary information when talking or writing about a client whether you are talking to the family doctor, the school principal, the probation officer, etc. Get to the point and report what is essential.

Records

If you keep any records of what is shared in the meetings, your client should know about it. Furthermore, you should be able to assure your client with integrity that the records are not available to his/her family or superiors. If, in the client's interest, you have to share material from the records, make sure you have the client's permission. Trust can be developed and maintained when confidentiality is guaranteed.

Bridging   This material on confidentiality applies to other relationships:
- Close friendships.
- Peers at work.
- Workshops and seminars.
- Wherever people need to trust you in order to tell you about themselves and their emotions.

Warning   You cannot be too careful about confidentiality. Watch yourself closely for every urge within you to tell somebody. If you need to talk with someone in order to settle down yourself, follow the advice on pp. 165 about the helper getting help.

WHEN NO ONE APPEARS TO NEED YOUR HELP

Focus

a. Qualified first aiders volunteer their services and no one seems to want or need their help.

b. There are potential clients with emotional problems and emergencies. Yet, there is no structure in the community to facilitate the client and first aider to get together.

c. The first aider is "only a volunteer" and does not feel that s/he has any authority. Hence the first aider is shy about offering services.

Illustrations   A. Albert has taken two courses in Emotional First Aid prior to moving to a new community. Being new, he has lots of free time. Formerly he had volunteered through a Pastoral Counselling Centre.

He doesn't know where to turn in this new community to offer his skills. Agencies like Pastoral Counselling and Family Service Centres do not exist.

B. Edna was called by a neighbor asking her to visit a friend whose husband has just left her and the small children. Edna's neighbor says that her friend is a very open person and it would be okay for Edna just to drop in without any formal introduction. By what authority does Edna make the visit.

Comments   There are several issues in these illustrations depicting some of the difficulties in getting together with potential clients.
- Some people think that they should be able to take care of themselves and do not easily ask for help.
- Some people insist on getting the best professional help and their first response is "a volunteer is not good enough."
- First aiders, particularly volunteers, often feel that they have no right or authority to be helping in this situation.

How to Solve these Problems

Training will help the first aider in understanding these problems and to gain skills in solving them.

In addition, or in the meantime, the first aider should contact one of the local agencies or organizations that has a structure for facilitating the first aider and the client to meet when the need arises.

The places to look for such facilitators are as follows:

Churches   Volunteer Action or Bureau
Hospital Auxiliary   Family Services
Pastoral Counselling   Family Life Centre
Local Mental Health Association
Local Crisis Line

Step by Step
Procedure 1. Read the sections in Chapter IV, Part One on achieving a relationship.

2. Give some thought to wherein lies your authority.
- The authority that comes through a recognized agency on whose behalf you act. e.g. Local Mental Health Association. Your church.
- The authority within you because of your training, your skills and motivation to help others help themselves.
- The authority the client gives you when s/he asks for help.
- The authority the client gives you when you agree on a contract or covenant.
- The authority the resistant client begins to give you as trust develops between you.

3. If you are a volunteer for a church or other agency, it helps if the sponsoring agency develops some means to let the community know that you act on their behalf: An article in the local newspaper. A designation ceremony as part of a regular church service.

4. When clients say that they really want a professional say something like "Maybe we can look together." Do not argue in an effort to prove your worth. As you look together, you can still help and the client may just decide that you are 'good enough'.

5. When clients feel shy about asking for help, say something like, "It's difficult for most people to ask for help."

6. If there is no organization in your community that facilitates clients and first aiders getting together, go out and round up one or two other interested citizens. Then talk about ways to solve the problem. Choose the most likely people, such as:
- other first aiders.
- persons who have status in the community. e.g. Doctor, clergy, alderman.
- persons who appreciate what first aiders can do.

7. Contact your local Mental Health Association, or pastor. They will consult with you about what you might do to solve the problem.

Bridging Chapter IV, Part One offers help in establishing the relationship once you are in contact with a client.

Warning Remember, as a first aider it's quality and not quantity that counts. In *one* situation you may help someone to help himself and life is forever richer for that person.

THE HELPER GETS HELP

The first responsibility of a helper in the field of emotional first aid is to himself/herself. You have a responsibility to attend to your own emotional life and to improve your skills.

Workshops and seminars will help with the skills, yet something more is needed in order "to avoid" getting stuck and/or emotionally burned-out, yourself.

The very best model for looking after yourself is to have easy access to a competent and caring mental health supervisor. The idea of 'supervisor' in this field differs from what most people in business and industry understand to be the role of the supervisor.

The role of the mental health supervisor is that of providing support as an equal. Granted the supervisor should have more experience and expertise than you. Remember though that you have some skills and lots of advantages that your supervisor may not have.

A good supervisor can be your "wailing wall", your confessor, and your encourager.

You can expect your mental health supervisor to utilize the same helping skills with you as outlined in this manual. If those skills are not at least as good as those outlined here, you need to get yourself a new supervisor.

If you are providing emotional first aid for people who are on the same payroll as you, then your supervisor should come from the outside, or from some non-partisan counsellor employed by the firm. If you have to avoid getting support because you are afraid of losing your client's trust, you leave yourself open to pain, disappointment and burn out. In short, do not box yourself into any helping situation where you are not free to turn for help yourself.

Do not wait until you are stuck with a client or are needing emotional first aid yourself. When you first begin meeting with clients is the right time to line up your supervisor.

Look around among the following list of professionals and do not settle for the first one you talk to; pick the best person for your needs.

The following professionals are among those most likely to have experience and training as mental health supervisors and/or consultants:

Pastoral counsellors   Psychologists
Social workers   Psychiatrists
Hospital chaplains

Another model for getting this kind of help and support is to form a group of peers who can provide peer supervision. If you go this route, it is important to invite a skilled professonal to the first meeting to help you get started. Furthermore, it is very important that you all work hard at keeping confidentiality. See Chapter V, section 6.

If you are having difficulty which you don't understand and the same difficulty tends to happen over and over again, you may need more than supervision. Find a competent helper and get your own therapy. You may have blind spots beneath your own awareness. Many of the most competent helpers have had their own therapy along the way.

REWARDING ENDING

Rewarding endings are to be cherished! The approach of *helping people to help themselves* has proved to be very satisfying for those professionals, volunteers and para-professionals who have learned the skills. You, as a first aider, can be one of them. The satisfaction comes through.

- Watching people grow,
- Watching people become stronger as they cope with their emotional struggles.

Some of the satisfactions come as surprises;

- A client's delight in discovering an inner strength.
- A first aider's delight in discovering that all you had to do was to be there as a caring person who shares the crisis.

There is currently a most important role for you in our society to help with;

- maintaining a high level of mental health in your community.
- improving the mental health of those people who suffer emotional pain and confusion.

That role will increase in the future. Some of the reasons for the increase are included in the section on Why Emotional First Aid is Important.

If you look after your own mental health, develop your skills and know your limitations, you will experience rewarding satisfaction as you help people to help themselves.

ORDER FORMS

Please send me _____ copy(ies) of the Emotional First Aid Manual   Date: _____

Name _____ Title/Position _____

Address _____ Organization _____

_____

_____ Postal/ZIP code

I have this to say about the Manual _____

_____

_____

_____

_____

_____. You may quote me: YES _____ NO _____

Please send me _____ copy(ies) of the Emotional First Aid Manual   Date: _____

Name _____ Title/Position _____

Address _____ Organization _____

_____

_____ Postal/ZIP code

I have this to say about the Manual _____

_____

_____

_____

_____. You may quote me: YES _____ NO _____

In the USA
Para-Professional Associates Int.
3820 190 pl, S.W.
Lynnwood, WA 98036
U.S.A.
Tel: (206) 778-8033

In Canada
Para-Professional Associates Int.
2104 Gordon Avenue
West Vancouver, B.C.
Canada V7V 1V9
Tel: (604) 926-5495

Copies are available also in Canada at offices of the **Canadian Mental Health Association.**

In Canada: $14.95 plus 1.25 postage/handling = $16.20 CD
In the U.S.A.: $12.95 plus 1.25 postage/handling = $14.20 US
Quantity discounts: 10-19 copies = 5%
                                      20-39 copies = 10%
                                      40 and more = 20%

Please send certified cheque
or money order.

Return policy:
Any single copy may be returned for a full refund of the book price within 30 days of shipping; the item must be received in re-saleable condition.
Quantity purchases may be returned only with written permission of the publisher.